Evo-Stik League Southern Supporters' Guide and Yearbook 2012

EDITOR
John Robinson

Second Edition

For details of our range of over 1,900 books and 400 DVDs, visit our web site or contact us using the information shown below.

British Library Cataloguing in Publication Data
A catalogue record for this book is available from the British Library

ISBN: 978-1-86223-223-5

Copyright © 2011, SOCCER BOOKS LIMITED (01472 696226)
72 St. Peter's Avenue, Cleethorpes, N.E. Lincolnshire, DN35 8HU, England
Web site   http://www.soccer-books.co.uk
e-mail   info@soccer-books.co.uk

All rights are reserved. No part of this publication may be reproduced, stored in a retrieval system or transmitted, in any form or by any means, electronic, mechanical, photocopying, recording, or otherwise, without the prior written permission of Soccer Books Limited.

The Publishers, and the Football Clubs itemised are unable to accept liability for any loss, damage or injury caused by error or inaccuracy in the information published in this guide.

Printed and bound in the UK by 4edge Ltd, Hockley.

FOREWORD

The "Supporters' Guide" series of books began life as "The Travelling Supporters' Guide" in 1982 and a separate guide covering the top two tiers of the Non-League pyramid has been published by Soccer Books Limited for almost 20 years! However, this is just the second edition of a Supporters' Guide dealing solely with the Southern Football League clubs and we hope that it is well received.

We have been unable to visit every ground in the course of preparing this guide and, as a consequence, we have been unable to obtain up-to-date ground photographs for all of the clubs. If any readers wish to send us suitable ground photographs for use in future editions of this guide, please contact us at the address shown on the facing page.

Where we use the term 'Child' for concessionary prices, this is often also the price charged to Senior Citizens.

The fixtures listed later in this book were released just a short time before we went to print and, as such, some of the dates shown may be subject to change. We therefore suggest that readers treat these fixtures as a rough guide and check dates carefully before attending matches.

Finally, we would like to wish our readers a safe and happy spectating season.

John Robinson
EDITOR

ACKNOWLEDGEMENTS

In the 6 months since we embarked upon the preparation of this guide, we have been greatly impressed by the cooperation extended to us by League officials and many individuals within the clubs themselves.

Consequently, our thanks go to the numerous club officials who have aided us in the compilation of information contained in this guide and also to Jason Mills of the Evo-Stik Southern Football League for his assistance. Our thanks also go to Michael Robinson (page layouts), Bob Budd (cover artwork), Tony Brown (Cup Statistics – www.soccerdata.com) and Dave Twydell and Derek Mead for providing some of the photographs. We would also like to thank:

Chris Bush – footballgroundz.co.uk
David Bauckham – davidbauckham.photoshelter.com
and Martin Wray – www.footballgroundsinfocus.com

for providing some of the other ground photographs used within this guide.

CONTENTS

The Evo-Stik League Southern Premier Division Club Information 6-28
The Evo-Stik League Southern Division One Central Club Information 29-51
The Evo-Stik League Southern Division One South & West Club Info. 52-73
Results for the Southern Football League Premier Division 2010/2011 74
Results for the Southern Football League Division One Central 2010/2011 75
Results for the Southern Football League Division One South & West 2010/11 ... 76
Southern Football League Premier Division
Final Table and Play-off Results 2010/2011 77
Southern Football League Division One Central and Division One South & West
Final Tables and Play-off Results 2010/2011 78
2010/2011 F.A. Trophy Results 79-84
2010/2011 F.A. Vase Results 85-89
England Internationals 2010-2011 90-91
Fixtures for The Evo-Stik League Southern Premier Division 2010/2011 92
Fixtures for The Evo-Stik League Southern Division One Central 2010/2011 93
Fixtures for The Evo-Stik League Southern Division One South & West 2010/11 94
Advertisement: Non-League Football Tables Series 95
Advertisement: The Supporters' Guide Series 96

THE EVO-STIK LEAGUE SOUTHERN PREMIER DIVISION

Secretary Jason Mills

Correspondence
secretary@southern-football-league.co.uk

Web Site www.southern-football-league.co.uk

Clubs for the 2011/2012 Season

AFC Totton	Page 7
Arlesey Town FC	Page 8
Banbury United FC	Page 9
Barwell FC	Page 10
Bashley FC	Page 11
Bedford Town FC	Page 12
Brackley Town FC	Page 13
Cambridge City FC	Page 14
Chesham United FC	Page 15
Chippenham Town FC	Page 16
Cirencester Town FC	Page 17
Evesham United FC	Page 18
Frome Town FC	Page 19
Hemel Hempstead Town FC	Page 20
Hitchin Town FC	Page 21
Leamington FC	Page 22
Oxford City FC	Page 23
Redditch United FC	Page 24
St. Albans City FC	Page 25
Stourbridge FC	Page 26
Swindon Supermarine FC	Page 27
Weymouth FC	Page 28

AFC TOTTON

Founded: 1886
Former Names: Totton FC
Nickname: 'The Stags'
Ground: Little Testwood Farm, Salisbury Road, Totton, Southampton
Record Attendance: Not applicable as the ground has yet to host a game

Colours: Blue shirts and shorts
Telephone N°: (023) 8086-8981 (Testwood Park number which may change for the new ground)
Ground Capacity: 2,000
Seating Capacity: 500
Web Site: www.afctotton.com
Contact E-mail: secretary@afctotton.com

GENERAL INFORMATION
Car Parking: At the Industrial Park adjacent to the ground
Coach Parking: At the ground
Nearest Railway Station: Totton (1½ miles)
Club Shop: At the ground
Opening Times: To be announced
Telephone N°: –

GROUND INFORMATION
Away Supporters' Entrances & Sections:
No usual segregation

ADMISSION INFO (2011/2012 PRICES)
Adult Standing: £9.00
Adult Seating: £9.00
Senior Citizen/Under-16s Standing: £4.00
Senior Citizen/Under-16s Seating: £4.00
Programme Price: £1.50

DISABLED INFORMATION
Wheelchairs: Accommodated
Helpers: Admitted
Prices: Normal prices apply for the disabled and helpers
Disabled Toilets: Available
Contact: Sean McGlead, c/o Club (Bookings are necessary)

Travelling Supporters' Information:
Routes: Exit the M27 at Junction 2 and head south on the A326. Almost immediately, take the slip road and turn left to join the A36 heading into Totton. The ground is located on the left hand side of the road after approximately ¾ mile, just before the roundabout for Calmore Industrial Park. Spectators travelling by car should turn left at this roundabout and can use the car park of Mansell Construction Services Ltd. which is immediately on the right after entering the Industrial Park.

ARLESEY TOWN FC

Founded: 1891
Former Names: None
Nickname: 'The Blues'
Ground: Armadillo Stadium, Hitchin Road, Arlesey, SG15 6RS
Record Attendance: 2,000 (1906)

Colours: Light and Dark Blue quartered shirts with Dark Blue shorts
Telephone Nº: (01462) 734504
Ground Capacity: 1,700
Seating Capacity: 150
Web Site: www.arleseyfc.co.uk

GENERAL INFORMATION
Car Parking: At the ground
Coach Parking: At the ground
Nearest Railway Station: Arlesey (1¾ miles)
Club Shop: In the Clubhouse at the ground
Opening Times: Evenings
Telephone Nº: (01462) 734504

GROUND INFORMATION
Away Supporters' Entrances & Sections:
No usual segregation

ADMISSION INFO (2011/2012 PRICES)
Adult Standing: £9.00
Adult Seating: £9.00
Senior Citizen/Junior Standing: £3.00
Senior Citizen/Junior Seating: £3.00
Programme Price: £1.50

DISABLED INFORMATION
Wheelchairs: Accommodated
Helpers: Admitted
Prices: Normal prices apply for the disabled and helpers
Disabled Toilets: Available in the Clubhouse
Contact: (01462) 734504   (Bookings are necessary)

Travelling Supporters' Information:
Routes: Exit the A1(M) at Junction 10 and take the A507 towards Stotford and Shefford. At the 3rd roundabout, take the first exit along Stotfold Road. Take the first turn on the left into House Lane which becomes the High Street and continue for approximately 1 mile. The ground is clearly visible on the left hand side of the road opposite the Hampden Business Centre.

BANBURY UNITED FC

Founded: 1931
Former Names: Spencer Villa FC and Banbury Spencer FC
Nickname: 'The Puritans'
Ground: Spencer Stadium, Station Approach, Banbury OX16 5AB
Record Attendance: 7,160 (vs Oxford City – 1948)

Pitch Size: 110 × 70 yards
Colours: Red and Gold shirts with Red shorts
Telephone Nº: (01295) 263354
Fax Number: (01295) 276492
Ground Capacity: 4,500
Seating Capacity: 250
Web site: www.banburyunited.co.uk

GENERAL INFORMATION
Car Parking: At the ground
Coach Parking: At the ground
Nearest Railway Station: Banbury (adjacent)
Nearest Bus Station: Banbury
Club Shop: At the ground
Opening Times: Matchdays only
Telephone Nº: (01295) 263354

GROUND INFORMATION
Away Supporters' Entrances & Sections:
No usual segregation

ADMISSION INFO (2011/2012 PRICES)
Adult Standing: £9.00
Adult Seating: £9.00
Senior Citizen Standing: £5.00
Senior Citizen Seating: £5.00
Under-16s Standing/Seating: £1.00
Programme Price: £2.00

DISABLED INFORMATION
Wheelchairs: 6 spaces available in total
Helpers: Admitted
Prices: Normal prices apply
Disabled Toilets: Available
Contact: (01295) 263354

Travelling Supporters' Information:
Routes: Exit the M40 at Junction 11 and head towards Banbury. Go straight on at the first roundabout then left at the next into Concorde Avenue. Continue straight on at the next roundabout then turn left at the traffic lights. Take the 1st turning on the right into Station Approach then take the single track road on the extreme right of the Station which leads to the Stadium.

BARWELL FC

Founded: 1992
Former Names: Formed by the amalgamation of Barwell Athletic FC and Hinckley FC in 1992
Nickname: 'The Canaries'
Ground: Kirkby Road Sports Ground, Kirkby Road, Barwell   LE9 8FQ
Record Attendance: 1,279

Colours: Yellow and Green shirts with Green shorts
Telephone Nº: (01455) 446048
Fax Number: (01455) 446048
Ground Capacity: 2,500
Seating Capacity: 256
Web Site: www.pitchero.com/clubs/barwell

GENERAL INFORMATION
Car Parking: At the ground
Coach Parking: At the ground
Nearest Railway Station: Hinckley (3¾ miles)
Club Shop: None
Opening Times: –
Telephone Nº: –

GROUND INFORMATION
Away Supporters' Entrances & Sections:
No usual segregation

ADMISSION INFO (2011/2012 PRICES)
Adult Standing: £8.00
Adult Seating: £8.00
Senior Citizen/Concessionary Standing: £5.00
Senior Citizen/Concessionary Seating: £5.00
Programme Price: £1.50

DISABLED INFORMATION
Wheelchairs: Accommodated
Helpers: Admitted
Prices: Normal prices apply for the disabled and helpers
Disabled Toilets: Available
Contact: (01455) 446048   (Bookings are not necessary)

Travelling Supporters' Information:
Routes: Exit the M69 at Junction 1 and take the A5 (Watling Street) towards Nuneaton. At the 3rd roundabout, take the 2nd exit onto the A47 (Dodwells Road) and follow to Barwell, crossing the A447. After crossing the A447, turn left at the roundabout and head into Barwell along The Common and follow into Chapel Street. Go straight on at the roundabout then turn immediately right along Kirkby Road. After approximately ¼ mile, the entrance to the ground is on the right, opposite the cemetery. The football ground itself is behind the cricket field.

BASHLEY FC

Founded: 1947
Former Names: None
Nickname: 'The Bash'
Ground: Bashley Road Ground, Bashley Road, New Milton BH25 5RY
Record Attendance: 3,500 (1987/88 season)

Colours: Gold shirts with Black shorts
Telephone Nº: (01425) 620280
Ground Capacity: 4,250
Seating Capacity: 250
Web Site: www.bashleyfc.co.uk

GENERAL INFORMATION
Car Parking: Available 100 yards from the ground
Coach Parking: At the ground
Nearest Railway Station: New Milton (1¼ miles)
Club Shop: At the ground
Opening Times: Matchdays only, open one hour before kick-off and also during half-time
Telephone Nº: (01425) 620280

GROUND INFORMATION
Away Supporters' Entrances & Sections:
No usual segregation

ADMISSION INFO (2011/2012 PRICES)
Adult Standing: £10.00
Adult Seating: £12.00
Concessionary Standing/Seating: £8.00
Note: Under-16s are admitted for £2.00 when accompanied by a paying adult
Programme Price: £1.50

DISABLED INFORMATION
Wheelchairs: Accommodated
Helpers: Admitted
Prices: Concessionary prices are charged for the disabled and helpers
Disabled Toilets: None
Contact: (01425) 620280   (Bookings are not necessary)

Travelling Supporters' Information:
Routes: The ground is located by the side of the B3058 in Bashley, just to the north of New Milton. Head southwards on the B3058 towards New Milton, bear right at the Rising Sun Public House and enter Bashley village. The ground is located on the left hand side of the road, shortly after passing the Esso petrol station.

BEDFORD TOWN FC

Founded: 1908 (Re-formed in 1989)
Former Names: None
Nickname: 'Eagles'
Ground: The Eyrie, Meadow Lane, Cardington, Bedford MK44 3SB
Record Attendance: 3,000 (6th August 1993)
Pitch Size: 110 × 72 yards

Colours: Shirts are Blue with White trim, Blue shorts
Telephone Nº: (01234) 831558
Fax Number: (01234) 831990
Ground Capacity: 3,000
Seating Capacity: 300
Web site: www.bedfordeagles.net
E-mail: david.swallow@bedfordeagles.net

GENERAL INFORMATION
Car Parking: At the ground
Coach Parking: At the ground
Nearest Railway Station: Bedford Midland (3 miles)
Nearest Bus Station: Greyfriars, Bedford (3 miles)
Club Shop: At the ground
Opening Times: Matchdays only
Telephone Nº: (01234) 831558

GROUND INFORMATION
Away Supporters' Entrances & Sections:
No usual segregation

ADMISSION INFO (2011/2012 PRICES)
Adult Standing: £9.00
Adult Seating: £9.00
Concessionary Standing: £6.00
Concessionary Seating: £6.00
Note: Under-13s are admitted for £2.00 if accompanied by a paying adult.
Programme Price: £1.50

DISABLED INFORMATION
Wheelchairs: Accommodated
Helpers: Admitted
Prices: Normal prices apply
Disabled Toilets: Available
Contact: (01234) 831558   (Bookings are not necessary)

Travelling Supporters' Information:
Routes: From the M1: Exit the M1 at Junction 13 onto the A421. Follow this the the bypass at the Sandy exit and take the A603 towards Sandy. The ground is on the left just before the lay-by; From the A1: Take the Sandy exit, go through Willington and the ground is on the right; From Bedford: Follow signs for Sandy and take Cardington Road out of town. The ground is on the left past 2 mini-roundabouts.

BRACKLEY TOWN FC

Founded: 1890
Former Names: None
Nickname: 'Saints'
Ground: St. James Park, Churchill Way, Brackley, NN13 7EJ
Record Attendance: 980 (2009/10 season)

Colours: Red and White striped shirts with Red shorts
Telephone Nº: (01280) 704077
Ground Capacity: 3,500
Seating Capacity: 300
Web Site: www.brackleytownfc.com

GENERAL INFORMATION
Car Parking: At the ground (£2.00 charge per car)
Coach Parking: At the ground
Nearest Railway Station: King's Sutton (6¾ miles)
Club Shop: At the ground
Opening Times: Matchdays and by appointment only
Telephone Nº: (01280) 704077

GROUND INFORMATION
Away Supporters' Entrances & Sections:
No usual segregation

ADMISSION INFO (2011/2012 PRICES)
Adult Standing/Seating: £8.00
Senior Citizen/Student Standing: £4.00
Senior Citizen/Student Seating: £4.00
Under-16s Standing/Seating: £2.00
Programme Price: £1.50

DISABLED INFORMATION
Wheelchairs: Accommodated
Helpers: Admitted
Prices: Normal prices apply for the disabled and helpers
Disabled Toilets: Available
Contact: (01280) 704077 (Stephen Toghill – bookings are necessary)

Travelling Supporters' Information:
Routes: From the West: Take the A422 to Brackley and take the first exit at the roundabout with the junction of the A43, heading north into Oxford Road.* Go straight on at the next roundabout and continue into Bridge Street before turning right into Churchill Way. The ground is located at the end of the road; From the South: Take the A43 northwards to Brackley. Take the second exit at the roundabout with the junction of the A422 and head into Oxford Road. Then as from * above; From the North-East: Take the A43 to Brackley. Upon reaching Brackley, take the 1st exit at the 1st roundabout, the 2nd exit at the next roundabout then the 3rd exit at the following roundabout into Oxford Road. Then as from * above.

CAMBRIDGE CITY FC

Founded: 1908
Former Names: Cambridge Town FC
Nickname: 'Lilywhites'
Ground: City Ground, Milton Road, Cambridge, CB4 1UY
Record Attendance: 12,058 (1950)
Pitch Size: 110 × 70 yards

Colours: White shirts with Black shorts
Telephone Nº: (01223) 357973
Fax Number: (01223) 351582
Ground Capacity: 2,300   **Seating Capacity:** 523
Correspondence: Andy Dewey, 50 Doggett Road, Cambridge   CB1 9LF
Web site: www.cambridgecityfc.com

GENERAL INFORMATION
Car Parking: 300 spaces available at the ground
Coach Parking: At the ground
Nearest Railway Station: Cambridge (2 miles)
Nearest Bus Station: Cambridge
Club Shop: At the ground
Opening Times: Matchdays only
Telephone Nº: (01223) 357973

GROUND INFORMATION
Away Supporters' Entrances & Sections:
No usual segregation

ADMISSION INFO (2011/2012 PRICES)
Adult Standing: £10.00   **Adult Seating:** £10.00
Concessionary Standing/Seating: £5.00
Under-16s Standing/Seating: £2.00
Note: Under-12s are admitted free of charge
Programme Price: £2.00

DISABLED INFORMATION
Wheelchairs: 6 spaces are available under cover on the half-way line
Helpers: Admitted
Prices: One helper admitted free with each disabled fan
Disabled Toilets: Two available in the Main Stand
Contact: (01223) 357973   (Bookings are not necessary)

Travelling Supporters' Information:
Routes: Exit the M11 at Junction 13 and take the A1303 into the City. At the end of Madingley Road, turn left into Chesterton Lane and then Chesterton Road. Go into the one-way system and turn left into Milton Road (A10) and the ground is on the left behind the Westbrook Centre.

CHESHAM UNITED FC

Founded: 1887
Former Names: Chesham Generals FC and Chesham Town FC
Nickname: 'The Generals'
Ground: The Meadow, Amy Lane, Chesham, Buckinghamshire HP5 1NE

Record Attendance: 5,000 (5th December 1979)
Colours: Claret shirts with Sky Blue shorts
Telephone Nº: (01494) 783964
Fax Number: (01494) 782456
Ground Capacity: 5,000   **Seating Capacity**: 250
Web site: www.cheshamunited.co.uk

GENERAL INFORMATION
Car Parking: At the ground
Coach Parking: At the ground
Nearest Railway Station: Chesham (½ mile)
Nearest Bus Station: Chesham (10 minutes walk)
Club Shop: At the ground
Opening Times: Matchdays only
Telephone Nº: (01494) 783964

GROUND INFORMATION
Away Supporters' Entrances & Sections:
No usual segregation

ADMISSION INFO (2011/2012 PRICES)
Adult Standing: £9.00
Adult Seating: £10.00
Under-16s Standing: £2.50 (Children under 6 free)
Under-16s Seating: £3.50 (Children under 6 free)
Senior Citizen/Student Standing: £5.50
Senior Citizen/Student Seating: £6.50
Programme Price: £1.70

DISABLED INFORMATION
Wheelchairs: Accommodated
Helpers: Admitted
Prices: Normal prices apply
Disabled Toilets: None
Contact: (01494) 783964   (Bookings are not necessary)

Travelling Supporters' Information:
Routes: The ground is situated on the A416. From the M40: Exit at Junction 2 (Beaconsfield) and follow signs to Amersham (A355) and then Chesham (A416). At the foot of the hill before entering town, turn sharp left at the roundabout for the ground; From the M25: Exit at Junction 20 (Abbot's Langley) and follow signs for the A41 (Aylesbury). Leave the A41 at the turn-off for Chesham, pass through Ashley Green until reaching Chesham. Pass through the town following signs for Amersham pass two garages then turn right at the roundabout for the ground; From the M1: Exit at Junction 8, follow signs to Hemel Hempstead then joing the A41 for Aylesbury. Then as above.

CHIPPENHAM TOWN FC

Founded: 1873
Former Names: None
Nickname: 'The Bluebirds'
Ground: Hardenhuish Park, Bristol Road, Chippenham, Wiltshire SN14 6LR
Record Attendance: 4,800 (1951)
Pitch Size: 110 × 70 yards

Colours: Royal Blue & White shirts, Royal Blue shorts
Telephone Nº: (01249) 650400
Contact Nº: (01249) 815516 (Football Secretary)
Fax Number: (01249) 650400
Ground Capacity: 3,000
Seating Capacity: 276
Web site: www.chippenhamtownfc.com

GENERAL INFORMATION
Car Parking: Adjacent to the ground
Coach Parking: At the ground
Nearest Railway Station: Chippenham (1 mile)
Nearest Bus Station: Chippenham
Club Shop: At the ground
Opening Times: Matchdays only
Telephone Nº: –

GROUND INFORMATION
Away Supporters' Entrances & Sections:
No usual segregation

ADMISSION INFO (2011/2012 PRICES)
Adult Standing: £8.00
Adult Seating: £9.00
Concessionary Standing: £5.00
Concessionary Seating: £6.00
Child Standing: £3.00
Child Seating: £4.00
Programme Price: £2.00

DISABLED INFORMATION
Wheelchairs: Accommodated at front of Stand
Helpers: Admitted
Prices: Normal prices apply for the disabled. Free for helpers
Disabled Toilets: None
Contact: (01249) 650400 (Bookings are not necessary)

Travelling Supporters' Information:
Routes: Exit the M4 at Junction 17 and take the A350. Turn right at the first roundabout and follow the road to the junction with the A420. Turn left following 'Town Centre' signs and the ground is just over ½ mile on the left near the Pelican crossing.

CIRENCESTER TOWN FC

Founded: 1889
Former Names: None
Nickname: 'Centurions'
Ground: Corinium Stadium, Kingshill Lane, Cirencester GL7 1HS
Record Attendance: 2,600 (vs Fareham – 1969)
Pitch Size: 110 × 70 yards

Colours: Red and Black shirts with Black shorts
Telephone Nº: (01285) 654543
Fax Number: (01285) 654474
Ground Capacity: 4,500
Seating Capacity: 550
Web site: www.cirentownfc.com

GENERAL INFORMATION
Car Parking: At the ground
Coach Parking: At the ground
Nearest Railway Station: Kemble (3 miles)
Nearest Bus Station: Cirencester (1 mile)
Club Shop: None

GROUND INFORMATION
Away Supporters' Entrances & Sections:
No usual segregation

ADMISSION INFO (2011/2012 PRICES)
Adult Standing: £8.00
Adult Seating: £8.00
Senior Citizen/Junior Standing: £5.00
Senior Citizen/Junior Seating: £5.00
Note: Admission is free for under 5s and Junior Members
Programme Price: £1.50

DISABLED INFORMATION
Wheelchairs: Accommodated
Helpers: Admitted
Prices: Normal prices apply
Disabled Toilets: Available in the Clubhouse
Contact: (01285) 654543

Travelling Supporters' Information:
Routes: Leave the Cirencester Bypass (A46) at the Burford Road roundabout following signs for Stow. Turn right at the traffic lights then right again at the junction. Take the 1st left into Kingshill Lane and the ground is situated about ¼ mile on the right.

EVESHAM UNITED FC

Evesham United FC are groundsharing with Worcester City FC until work on their new ground is completed. Please contact the club for further information.

Founded: 1945
Former Names: Evesham Town FC
Nickname: 'The Robins'
Ground: St. Georges Lane, Worcester WR1 1QT
Record Attendance: –
Pitch Size: 110 × 75 yards

Colours: Red and White striped shirts, White shorts
Telephone Nº: (01905) 23003
Fax Number: (01905) 26668
Ground Capacity: 4,500
Seating Capacity: 1,100
Web site: www.eveshamunitedfc.com

GENERAL INFORMATION
Car Parking: Street parking
Coach Parking: Street parking
Nearest Railway Station: Foregate Street (1 mile)
Nearest Bus Station: Crowngate Bus Station
Club Shop: At the ground
Opening Times: Matchdays only
Telephone Nº: –

GROUND INFORMATION
Away Supporters' Entrances & Sections:
Turnstile at the Canal End when segregation is in force for Canal End accommodation

ADMISSION INFO (2011/2012 PRICES)
Adult Standing: £8.00
Adult Seating: £8.00
Senior Citizen/Junior Standing: £4.00
Senior Citizen/Junior Seating: £4.00
Programme Price: £1.50

DISABLED INFORMATION
Wheelchairs: Accommodated
Helpers: Admitted
Prices: Standard prices apply
Disabled Toilets: Available
Contact: (01684) 561770 (Mike Peplow – Football Secretary)

Travelling Supporters' Information:
Routes: Exit the M5 at Junction 6 and take the A449 Kidderminster Road. Follow to the end of the dual carriageway and take the second exit at the roundabout for Worcester City Centre. At the first set of traffic lights turn right into the town centre. The 3rd turning on the left is St. Georges Lane.

FROME TOWN FC

Founded: 1904
Former Names: None
Nickname: 'The Robins'
Ground: Aldersmith Stadium, Badgers Hill, Berkley Road, Frome   BA11 2EH
Record Attendance: 8,000 (1954)

Colours: Red shirts and shorts
Telephone Nº: (01373) 464087
Fax Number: (01373) 464087
Ground Capacity: 2,000
Seating Capacity: 150
Web Site: www.frometownfc.co.uk

GENERAL INFORMATION
Car Parking: At the ground
Coach Parking: At the ground
Nearest Railway Station: Frome (1 mile)
Club Shop: At the ground
Opening Times: Matchdays only
Telephone Nº: –

GROUND INFORMATION
Away Supporters' Entrances & Sections:
No usual segregation

ADMISSION INFO (2011/2012 PRICES)
Adult Standing/Seating: £10.00
Senior Citizen/Concessions Standing/Seating: £6.00
Under-16s Standing/Seating: £3.00
Note: Under-12s are admitted free when accompanied by a paying adult
Programme Price: £1.50

DISABLED INFORMATION
Wheelchairs: Accommodated
Helpers: Admitted
Prices: Normal prices apply for the disabled and helpers
Disabled Toilets: None
Contact: (01373) 464087   (Bookings are necessary)

Travelling Supporters' Information:
Routes: Take the A36 southwards from Bath and, after passing Beckington, join the A361 heading towards Frome. At the next roundabout, join the B3090 and continue into Frome from the north. Turn left into Berkley Road shortly after passing the Cricket Ground on the left and Aldersmith Stadium is on the right hand side after a short distance.

HEMEL HEMPSTEAD TOWN FC

Founded: 1885
Former Names: Apsley FC and Hemel Hempstead FC
Nickname: 'The Tudors'
Ground: Vauxhall Road, Adeyfield, Hemel Hempstead HP2 4HW
Record Attendance: 2,000 (vs Watford – 1985)
Pitch Size: 112 × 72 yards
Colours: Shirts and Shorts are Red with White trim
Telephone Nº: (01442) 259777
Fax Number: (01442) 264322
Ground Capacity: 2,500
Seating Capacity: 350
Web site: www.hemelfc.com

GENERAL INFORMATION
Car Parking: At the ground
Coach Parking: At the ground
Nearest Railway Station: Hemel Hempstead (1½ miles)
Nearest Bus Station: Hemel Hempstead (¾ mile)
Club Shop: None

GROUND INFORMATION
Away Supporters' Entrances & Sections:
No usual segregation

ADMISSION INFO (2011/2012 PRICES)
Adult Standing: £8.00
Adult Seating: £8.00
Concessionary Standing/Seating: £5.00
Junior Standing/Seating: £1.00
Programme Price: £2.00

DISABLED INFORMATION
Wheelchairs: Accommodated
Helpers: Admitted
Prices: Normal prices apply
Disabled Toilets: Available in the Clubhouse
Contact: (01442) 259777

Travelling Supporters' Information:
Routes: Exit the M1 at Junction 8 and go straight ahead at the first roundabout. When approaching the 2nd roundabout move into the right hand lane and, as you continue straight across be ready to turn right almost immediately through a gap in the central reservation. This turn-off is Leverstock Green Road and continue along this to the double mini-roundabout. At this roundabout turn left into Vauxhall Road and the ground is on the right at the next roundabout.

HITCHIN TOWN FC

Founded: 1865 (Re-formed in 1928)
Former Names: Hitchin FC
Nickname: 'The Canaries'
Ground: Top Field, Fishponds Road, Hitchin, Hertfordshire SG5 1NU
Record Attendance: 7,878 (1956)
Ground Capacity: 4,554   **Seating Capacity**: 500

Pitch Size: 114 × 78 yards
Colours: Yellow shirts with Green shorts
Telephone Nº: (01462) 434483 (Club)
Daytime Phone Nº: (01767) 315350
Matchday Phone Nº: (01462) 459028
Fax Number: (01462) 638718
Web site: www.hitchintownfc.co.uk

GENERAL INFORMATION
Car Parking: Space for 200 cars at the ground
Coach Parking: At the ground
Nearest Railway Station: Hitchin (1 mile)
Club Shop: At the ground
Opening Times: Matchdays only
Telephone Nº: None

GROUND INFORMATION
Away Supporters' Entrances & Sections:
No usual segregation

ADMISSION INFO (2011/2012 PRICES)
Adult Standing/Seating: £9.00
Concessionary Standing/Seating: £5.00
Under-17s Standing/Seating: £1.00
Programme Price: £2.00

DISABLED INFORMATION
Wheelchairs: 10 spaces are available by the Main Stand
Helpers: Admitted
Prices: Normal prices apply
Disabled Toilets: Available at rear of the Main Stand
Contact: (01462) 434483 or (01767) 315350 (Please book)

Travelling Supporters' Information:
Routes: Take A1(M) to Junction 8 and follow A602 signposted to Hitchin. At Three Moorhens roundabout, take 3rd exit onto A600 towards Bedford. At next roundabout go straight over onto one-way system, go straight over at traffic lights, turn right at next roundabout and the turnstiles are immediately on the left. The Car Park turning is 50 yards further on; Alternatively, take M1 to Junction 10 and follow well appointed signs to Hitchin via A505. On approach to Hitchin go straight over initial mini-roundabout, turn left at next roundabout and turnstiles are situated immediately on the left; By Train: From Hitchin Station turn right outside station approach and follow the road around the DIY store into Nightingale Road which leads past the Woolpack Pub to The Victoria. Take Bunyan Road at The Victoria which leads into Fishponds Road.

LEAMINGTON FC

Founded: 1891
Former Names: Leamington Town FC, Lockheed Borg & Beck FC, AP Leamington FC and Lockheed Leamington FC
Nickname: 'The Brakes'
Ground: New Windmill Ground, Harbury Lane, Whitnash, Leamington CV33 9JR

Record Attendance: 1,380 (17th February 2007)
Colours: Gold and Black shirts with Black shorts
Telephone Nº: (01926) 430406
Fax Number: (01926) 430406
Ground Capacity: 5,000
Seating Capacity: 120
Web Site: www.leamingtonfc.co.uk

GENERAL INFORMATION
Car Parking: At the ground
Coach Parking: At the ground
Nearest Railway Station: Leamington (4 miles)
Club Shop: At the ground
Opening Times: Matchdays only
Telephone Nº: –

GROUND INFORMATION
Away Supporters' Entrances & Sections:
No usual segregation

ADMISSION INFO (2011/2012 PRICES)
Adult Standing/Seating: £9.00
Concessionary Standing/Seating: £6.00
Under-16s Standing/Seating: £3.00 (Under-12s free)
Programme Price: £2.00

DISABLED INFORMATION
Wheelchairs: Accommodated
Helpers: Admitted
Prices: Normal prices apply for the disabled. Helpers are admitted free of charge
Disabled Toilets: Available
Contact: (01926) 430406 (Bookings are not necessary)

Travelling Supporters' Information:
Routes: Exit the M40 at Junction 14 and take the A452 towards Leamington continuing at the roundabout into Europa Way (still A452). After approximately ½ mile, take the 4th exit at the roundabout into Harbury Lane (signposted for Harbury and Bishops Tachbrook). Continue on Harbury lane, taking the 3rd exit at the first roundabout and going straight ahead at the traffic lights. The ground is on the left hand side of the road after approximately 1½ miles.

OXFORD CITY FC

Founded: 1882
Former Names: None
Nickname: 'City'
Ground: Court Place Farm, Marsh Lane, Marston, Oxford OX3 0NQ
Record Attendance: 9,500 (1950)

Colours: Blue & White hooped shirts with Blue shorts
Telephone No: (01865) 744493
Ground Capacity: 3,000
Seating Capacity: 300
Web Site: www.oxfordcityfc.co.uk

GENERAL INFORMATION
Car Parking: At the ground
Coach Parking: At the ground
Nearest Railway Station: Oxford (3¾ miles)
Club Shop: At the ground
Opening Times: Matchdays only
Telephone No: (01865) 744493

GROUND INFORMATION
Away Supporters' Entrances & Sections:
No usual segregation

ADMISSION INFO (2011/2012 PRICES)
Adult Standing/Seating: £9.00
Concessionary Standing/Seating: £4.50
Under-16s Standing/Seating: Free of charge
Programme Price: £1.50

DISABLED INFORMATION
Wheelchairs: Accommodated
Helpers: Admitted
Prices: Normal prices apply for the disabled and helpers
Disabled Toilets: Available
Contact: (01865) 744493 (Bookings are not necessary)

Travelling Supporters' Information:
Routes: The stadium is located by the side of the A40 Northern Bypass Road next to the Marston flyover junction to the north east of Oxford. Exit the A40 at the Marston junction and head into Marsh Lane (B4150). Take the first turn on the left into the OXSRAD Complex then turn immediately left again to follow the approach road to the stadium in the far corner of the site.

REDDITCH UNITED FC

Founded: 1891
Former Names: Redditch Town FC
Nickname: 'The Reds'
Ground: Valley Stadium, Bromsgrove Road, Redditch B97 4RN
Record Attendance: 5,500 (vs Bromsgrove 1954/55)
Pitch Size: 110 × 72 yards

Colours: Red shirts, shorts and socks
Telephone Nº: (01527) 67450
Contact Nº: (01527) 67450
Fax Number: (01527) 67450
Ground Capacity: 3,500
Seating Capacity: 516
Web site: www.redditchutdfc.co.uk

GENERAL INFORMATION
Supporters Club: c/o Club
Telephone Nº: (01527) 67450
Car Parking: At the ground
Coach Parking: At the ground
Nearest Railway Station: Redditch (¼ mile)
Nearest Bus Station: Redditch (¼ mile)
Club Shop: At the ground
Opening Times: Matchdays only

GROUND INFORMATION
Away Supporters' Entrances & Sections:
No segregation

ADMISSION INFO (2011/2012 PRICES)
Adult Standing: £9.00
Adult Seating: £10.00
Senior Citizen/Concessionary Standing: £5.00
Senior Citizen/Concessionary Seating: £6.00
Under-16s Standing: £1.00
Under-16s Seating: £2.00
Family Ticket: £12.00 (2 adults + 2 children – only available for certain matches, however)
Programme Price: £2.00

DISABLED INFORMATION
Wheelchairs: Accommodated
Helpers: Admitted
Prices: Normal prices apply to both helpers and disabled
Disabled Toilets: Available
Contact: (01527) 67450 (Bookings are not necessary)

Travelling Supporters' Information:
Routes: Exit the M42 at Junction 2 and follow the A441 towards Redditch. Upon reaching the outskirts of Reddith, take the 4th exit at the roundabout (signposted Batchley) then turn left at the traffic lights into Birmingham Road. Take the next right into Clive Road then left into Hewell Road. Continue to the T-junction and turn right, passing the Railway Station on the right. Continue through the traffic lights and entrance to the ground is situated on the right hand side after about ¼ mile.

ST. ALBANS CITY FC

Founded: 1908
Former Names: None
Nickname: 'The Saints'
Ground: Clarence Park, York Road, St. Albans, Hertfordshire AL1 4PL
Record Attendance: 9,757 (27th February 1926)
Pitch Size: 110 × 80 yards

Colours: Blue shirts with Yellow trim, Yellow shorts
Telephone Nº: (01727) 864296
Fax Number: (01727) 866235
Ground Capacity: 5,007
Seating Capacity: 667
Web site: www.sacfc.co.uk

GENERAL INFORMATION
Car Parking: Street parking
Coach Parking: In Clarence Park
Nearest Railway Station: St. Albans City (200 yds)
Club Shop: At the ground
Opening Times: Matchdays only
Telephone Nº: (01727) 864296

GROUND INFORMATION
Away Supporters' Entrances & Sections:
Hatfield Road End when matches are segregated

ADMISSION INFO (2011/2012 PRICES)
Adult Standing: £10.00   **Adult Seating**: £12.00
Senior Citizens/Under-16s Standing: £5.00
Senior Citizens/Under-16s Seating: £6.00
Under-12s Standing/Seating: £2.00   (Under-5s free)
Programme Price: £2.50

DISABLED INFORMATION
Wheelchairs: Accommodated
Helpers: One admitted per disabled supporter
Prices: Free for disabled, concessionary prices for helpers
Disabled Toilets: Available in the York Road End
Contact: (01727) 864296   (Bookings are not necessary)

Travelling Supporters' Information:
Routes: Take the M1 or M10 to the A405 North Orbital Road and at the roundabout at the start of the M10, go north on the A5183 (Watling Street). Turn right along St. Stephen's Hill and carry along into St. Albans. Continue up Holywell Hill, go through two sets of traffic lights and at the end of St. Peter's Street, take a right turn at the roundabout into Hatfield Road. Follow over the mini-roundabouts and at the second set of traffic lights turn left into Clarence Road and the ground is on the left. Park in Clarence Road and enter the ground via the Park or in York Road and use the entrance by the footbridge.

STOURBRIDGE FC

Founded: 1876
Former Names: Stourbridge Standard FC
Nickname: 'The Glassboys'
Ground: War Memorial Ground, High Street, Amblecote, Stourbridge DY8 4HN
Record Attendance: 5,726 (1974)

Colours: Red and White striped shirts with Red shorts
Telephone Nº: (01384) 394040
Ground Capacity: 2,000
Seating Capacity: 250
Web Site: www.stourbridgefc.com
E-mail: admin@stourbridgefc.com

GENERAL INFORMATION
Car Parking: At the ground
Coach Parking: Please contact the club for information
Nearest Railway Station: Stourbridge Town (¾ mile)
Club Shop: At the ground
Opening Times: Matchdays only from 1 hour before kick-off
Telephone Nº: (01384) 394040

GROUND INFORMATION
Away Supporters' Entrances & Sections:
No usual segregation

ADMISSION INFO (2011/2012 PRICES)
Adult Standing/Seating: £9.00
Senior Citizen Standing/Seating: £5.00
Under-16s Standing/Seating: £4.00
Note: Under-11s are admitted free of charge when accompanied by a paying adult
Programme Price: £1.50

DISABLED INFORMATION
Wheelchairs: Accommodated
Helpers: Admitted
Prices: Normal prices apply for the disabled and helpers
Disabled Toilets:
Contact: (01384) 394040   (Bookings are necessary)

Travelling Supporters' Information:
Routes: From the South: Exit the M5 at Junction 4 and take the A491 to Stourbridge. Continue along the A491, pass Hagley then go through Pedmore and Old Swinford before joining the Stourbridge Ring Road (one-way). Follow the lane signs for Wolverhampton A491. Pass through three sets of traffic lights before reaching the ground which is on the left hand side of the road, opposite the Royal Oak Public House; From the North or East: Exit the M5 at Junction 3 and take the A456 towards Stourbridge and Kidderminster. After about five miles, turn right at the traffic lights in Hagley to join the A491 and follow into Stourbridge passing through Pedmore and Old Swinford onto the Stourbridge Ring-Road (one-way) as above.

SWINDON SUPERMARINE FC

Founded: 1992
Former Names: None
Nickname: 'Marine'
Ground: Hunts Copse, Supermarine Road, Swindon, SN3 4SZ
Record Attendance: 1,550

Colours: Blue and White shirts with Blue shorts
Telephone Nº: (01793) 828778
Fax Number: (01793) 790865
Ground Capacity: 3,000
Seating Capacity: 345
Web Site: www.swindonsupermarinefc.com

GENERAL INFORMATION
Car Parking: 200 spaces at the ground (£1.00 charge per car)
Coach Parking: At the ground
Nearest Railway Station: Swindon (4 miles)
Club Shop: At the ground
Opening Times: Matchdays only
Telephone Nº: (01793) 828778

GROUND INFORMATION
Away Supporters' Entrances & Sections:
No usual segregation

ADMISSION INFO (2011/2012 PRICES)
Adult Standing: £9.00   Adult Seating: £9.00
Senior Citizen/Under-16s Standing: £5.00
Senior Citizen/Under-16s Seating: £5.00
Family Tickets: £25.00
Note: Under-11s are admitted free of charge when accompanied by a paying adult
Programme Price: £1.50

DISABLED INFORMATION
Wheelchairs: Accommodated
Helpers: Admitted
Prices: Normal prices apply for the disabled and helpers
Disabled Toilets: Available
Contact: (01793) 828778   (Bookings are not necessary)

Travelling Supporters' Information:
Routes: The ground is located next to the South Marston Industrial Estate just off the A361 to the north of Swindon and south of Highworth. Follow the signs for the Industrial Estate then turn into Supermarine Road at the roundabout to the north of the industrial estate. The ground is on the left hand side of the road, opposite the industrial estate.

WEYMOUTH FC

Founded: 1890
Former Names: None
Nickname: 'Terras'
Ground: Wessex Stadium, Radipole Lane, Weymouth, Dorset DT4 9XJ
Record Attendance: 6,500 (14th November 2005)

Colours: Shirts are Claret and Sky Blue, Claret shorts
Telephone Nº: 08721 840000
Fax Number: (0117) 327-0298
Ground Capacity: 6,500
Seating Capacity: 800
Web site: www.theterras.co.uk

GENERAL INFORMATION
Car Parking: 200 spaces available at the ground
Coach Parking: At the ground
Nearest Railway Station: Weymouth (2 miles)
Nearest Bus Station: Weymouth Town Centre
Club Shop: At the ground
Opening Times: Matchdays only
Telephone Nº: –

GROUND INFORMATION
Away Supporters' Entrances & Sections:
No usual segregation

ADMISSION INFO (2011/2012 PRICES)
Adult Standing: £11.00
Adult Seating: £11.00
Senior Citizen/Student Standing: £8.00
Senior Citizen/Student Seating: £8.00
Under-16s Standing: £3.00
Under-16s Seating: £3.00
Programme Price: –

DISABLED INFORMATION
Wheelchairs: Accommodated
Helpers: Admitted
Prices: Normal prices apply for the disabled. Free for helpers
Disabled Toilets: Yes
Contact: (01305) 785558   (Bookings are not necessary)

Travelling Supporters' Information:
Routes: Take the A354 from Dorchester to Weymouth and turn right at the first roundabout to the town centre. Take the 3rd exit at the next roundabout and follow signs for the ground which is about ½ mile on the right.

THE EVO-STIK LEAGUE SOUTHERN DIVISION ONE CENTRAL

Secretary Jason Mills

Correspondence secretary@southern-football-league.co.uk

Web Site www.southern-football-league.co.uk

Clubs for the 2011/2012 Season

AFC Hayes	Page 30
Ashford Town (Middlesex) FC	Page 31
Aylesbury FC	Page 32
Barton Rovers FC	Page 33
Beaconsfield SYCOB FC	Page 34
Bedfont Town FC	Page 35
Bedworth United FC	Page 36
Biggleswade Town FC	Page 37
Burnham FC	Page 38
Chalfont St. Peter FC	Page 39
Chertsey Town FC	Page 40
Daventry Town FC	Page 41
Fleet Town FC	Page 42
Leighton Town FC	Page 43
Marlow FC	Page 44
North Greenford United FC	Page 45
Northwood FC	Page 46
Rugby Town FC	Page 47
Slough Town FC	Page 48
St. Neots Town FC	Page 49
Uxbridge FC	Page 50
Woodford United FC	Page 51

AFC HAYES

Founded: 1974
Former Names: Brook House FC
Nickname: 'The Brook'
Ground: Farm Park, Kingshill Avenue, Hayes, UB4 8DD
Record Attendance: 1,800 (vs Chelsea in the Middlesex Cup)

Colours: Blue and White striped shirts with Blue shorts
Telephone Nº: (020) 8845-0110
Fax Number: (020) 8842-1448
Ground Capacity: 2,000
Seating Capacity: 150
Web Site: www.pitchero.com/clubs/afchayes

GENERAL INFORMATION
Car Parking: At the ground
Coach Parking: At the ground
Nearest Railway Station: South Ruislip (1¾ miles)
Nearest Tube Station: South Ruislip (3 miles)
Club Shop: None
Opening Times: –
Telephone Nº: –

GROUND INFORMATION
Away Supporters' Entrances & Sections:
No usual segregation

ADMISSION INFO (2011/2012 PRICES)
Adult Standing: £8.00
Adult Seating: £8.00
Senior Citizen/Junior Standing: £4.00
Senior Citizen/Junior Seating: £4.00
Programme Price: £1.00

DISABLED INFORMATION
Wheelchairs: Accommodated
Helpers: Admitted
Prices: Normal prices apply for the disabled and helpers
Disabled Toilets: None
Contact: (020) 8845-0110 (Bookings are not necessary)

Travelling Supporters' Information:
Routes: Take the A40 (Western Avenue) to the McDonalds Target roundabout then join the A312 heading south towards Hayes. At the White Hart roundabout, take the 3rd exit into Yeading Lane then turn right at the first set of traffic lights into Kingshill Avenue. The ground is on the right after about a mile.

ASHFORD TOWN (MIDDLESEX) FC

Founded: 1964
Former Names: Formed following the demise of Ashford Albion FC
Nickname: 'Tangerines'
Ground: Short Lane Stadium, Short Lane, Stanwell, Staines TW19 7BH
Record Attendance: 992 vs AFC Wimbledon (2006)
Pitch Size: 111 × 73 yards
Colours: Tangerine and White striped shirts with Black shorts
Telephone Nº: (01784) 245908
Fax Number: (01784) 253913
Ground Capacity: 2,550
Seating Capacity: 250
Web site: www.ashfordtownmiddlesexfc.com

GENERAL INFORMATION
Car Parking: At the ground
Coach Parking: At the ground
Nearest Railway Station: Ashford (Middlesex) (1 mile)
Nearest Tube Station: Hatton Cross (3 miles)
Club Shop: At the ground
Opening Times: Daily
Telephone Nº: (01784) 245908

GROUND INFORMATION
Away Supporters' Entrances & Sections:
No usual segregation

ADMISSION INFO (2011/2012 PRICES)
Adult Standing/Seating: £9.00
Senior Citizen/Student Standing/Seating: £5.00
Under-16s Standing/Seating: £1.00
Programme Price: £2.00

DISABLED INFORMATION
Wheelchairs: Accommodated
Helpers: Admitted
Prices: Free of charge for the disabled
Disabled Toilets: Available
Contact: (01784) 245908   (Bookings are not necessary)

Travelling Supporters' Information:
Routes: Exit the M25 at Junction 13 and follow the A30 towards London. After passing Ashford Hospital on the left, take the 3rd turning on the left into Short Lane (adjacent to the footbridge) and the ground is on the right hand side after ¼ mile.

AYLESBURY FC

Founded: 1930 (As Stocklake FC)
Former Names: Stocklake FC, Belgrave FC, Haywood United FC and Aylesbury Vale FC
Nickname: 'The Moles'
Ground: Haywood Way, Aylesbury HP19 9WZ
Record Attendance: 250

Colours: Red and Black shirts with Black shorts
Telephone Nº: (01296) 421101
Fax Number: (01296) 421101
Ground Capacity: 1,000
Seating Capacity: 50
Web Site: www.aylesburyfootballclub.co.uk

GENERAL INFORMATION
Car Parking: Limited number of spaces at the ground
Coach Parking: At the ground
Nearest Railway Station: Aylesbury (2 miles)
Club Shop: Via the Club's web site only
Opening Times: –
Telephone Nº: –

GROUND INFORMATION
Away Supporters' Entrances & Sections:
No usual segregation

ADMISSION INFO (2011/2012 PRICES)
Adult Standing: £7.00
Adult Seating: £7.00
Senior Citizen Standing: £5.00
Senior Citizen Seating: £5.00
Under-16s Standing/Seating: £1.00
Note: Ticket prices may vary for Cup matches
Programme Price: £1.50

DISABLED INFORMATION
Wheelchairs: Accommodated
Helpers: Admitted
Prices: Normal prices apply for the disabled and helpers
Disabled Toilets: Available
Contact: (01296) 421101   (Bookings are not necessary)

Travelling Supporters' Information:
Routes: Take the A41 (Bicester Road) to the north-western outskirts of Aylesbury near to Rabans Lane Industrial Estate. Turn into Jackson Road at the roundabout at the edge of town and Haywood Way is the 2nd turning on the left. The ground is at the end of the lane.

BARTON ROVERS FC

Founded: 1898
Former Names: None
Nickname: 'Rovers'
Ground: Sharpenhoe Road, Barton-le-Clay, MK45 4SD
Record Attendance: 1,900 (1976)

Colours: Yellow shirts with Black shorts
Telephone Nº: (01582) 707772
Fax Number: (01582) 707772
Ground Capacity: 4,000
Seating Capacity: 160
Web Site: www.bartonrovers.co.uk

GENERAL INFORMATION
Car Parking: At the ground
Coach Parking: At the ground
Nearest Railway Station: Harlington (3½ miles)
Club Shop: None
Opening Times: –
Telephone Nº: –

GROUND INFORMATION
Away Supporters' Entrances & Sections:
No usual segregation

ADMISSION INFO (2011/2012 PRICES)
Adult Standing: £8.00
Adult Seating: £8.00
Senior Citizen/Junior Standing: £5.00
Senior Citizen/Junior Seating: £5.00
Programme Price: £1.50

DISABLED INFORMATION
Wheelchairs: Accommodated
Helpers: Admitted
Prices: Normal prices apply for the disabled and helpers
Disabled Toilets: Available
Contact: (01582) 707772 (Bookings are necessary)

Travelling Supporters' Information:
Routes: The ground is located in Barton-le-Clay which is about 5 miles to the north of Luton by the side of the A6 road. Take the A6 to Barton-le-Clay and exit at the roundabout onto the B655 into Barton itself. Continue along the B655 Bedford Road then turn right at the mini-roundabout into Sharpenhoe Road. The entrance to the ground is on the left just after the houses.

BEACONSFIELD SYCOB FC

Founded: 1994
Former Names: Formed by the amalgamation of Beaconsfield United FC and Slough YCOB FC
Nickname: 'The Rams'
Ground: Holloways Park, Windsor Road, Beaconsfield HP9 2SE
Record Attendance: 3,000 (1985)

Colours: Red & White quartered shirts, Black shorts
Telephone Nº: (01494) 676868
Fax Number: (01753) 865081
Ground Capacity: 3,000
Seating Capacity: 250
Web site: www.beaconsfieldsycobfc.com

GENERAL INFORMATION
Car Parking: At the ground
Coach Parking: At the ground
Nearest Railway Station: Beaconsfield (2½ miles)
Club Shop: At the ground
Opening Times: Matchdays only
Telephone Nº: (01494) 676868

GROUND INFORMATION
Away Supporters' Entrances & Sections:
No usual segregation

ADMISSION INFO (2011/2012 PRICES)
Adult Standing: £7.50
Adult Seating: £7.50
Senior Citizen/Junior Standing: £4.00
Senior Citizen/Junior Seating: £4.00
Programme Price: £2.00

DISABLED INFORMATION
Wheelchairs: Accommodated
Helpers: Admitted
Prices: Normal prices apply for the disabled and helpers
Disabled Toilets: Available
Contact: (01494) 676868 (Bookings are not necessary)

Travelling Supporters' Information:
Routes: Exit the M40 at Junction 2 and head into the Beaconsfield Motorway Service area. In the services, follow the signs for Beaconsfield SYCOB, crossing the A355 and heading back towards the M40. After approximately 150 yards turn left into the ground and the car park and Clubhouse are on the right after 200 yards.

BEDFONT TOWN FC

Founded: 1965
Former Names: Bedfont Green FC
Nickname: 'The Peacocks'
Ground: The Orchard, Hatton Road, Bedfont, TW14 9QT
Record Attendance: 259 (18th August 2010)

Colours: Navy Blue shirts and White shorts
Telephone No: (020) 8890-7264
Ground Capacity: 1,200
Seating Capacity: 150
Web Site: www.bedfonttownfc.co.uk

GENERAL INFORMATION
Car Parking: At the ground
Coach Parking: At the ground
Nearest Railway Station: Heathrow Terminal 4 (1 mile)
Nearest Tube Station: Hatton Cross (½ mile)
Club Shop: None at present
Opening Times: –
Telephone No: –

GROUND INFORMATION
Away Supporters' Entrances & Sections:
Segregation is only in place on rare occasions – please contact the club for further details

ADMISSION INFO (2011/2012 PRICES)
Adult Standing: £8.00
Adult Seating: £8.00
Senior Citizen/Junior Standing: £4.00
Senior Citizen/Junior Seating: £4.00
Programme Price: £2.00

DISABLED INFORMATION
Wheelchairs: Accommodated
Helpers: Admitted
Prices: Concessionary prices are charged for the disabled and helpers
Disabled Toilets: Available
Contact: (020) 8890-7264 (Bookings are not necessary)

Travelling Supporters' Information:
Routes: The ground is located just next to Heathrow Airport southern perimeter. Take the A30 Great South-West Road and turn south into Hatton Road at the junction next to Hatton Cross Tube station. Turn immediately right to continue along Hatton Road and the ground is on the left hand side of the road after approximately ½ mile.

BEDWORTH UNITED FC

Founded: 1895
Former Names: Bedworth Town FC
Nickname: 'The Greenbacks'
Ground: The Oval, Miners Welfare Park, Coventry Road, Bedworth CV12 8NN
Record Attendance: 5,127 (23rd February 1982)

Colours: Green shirts and shorts
Telephone Nº: (02476) 314752
Ground Capacity: 7,000
Seating Capacity: 300
Web Site: www.bedworthunited.co.uk

GENERAL INFORMATION
Car Parking: Limited number of spaces available at the ground and Town Centre car parks are a short walk
Coach Parking: At the ground
Nearest Railway Station: Bedworth (¼ mile)
Club Shop: At the ground
Opening Times: Matchdays only
Telephone Nº: (02476) 314752

GROUND INFORMATION
Away Supporters' Entrances & Sections:
No usual segregation

ADMISSION INFO (2011/2012 PRICES)
Adult Standing: £7.00
Adult Seating: £7.00
Senior Citizen/Junior Standing: £4.00
Senior Citizen/Junior Seating: £4.00
Programme Price: £1.00

DISABLED INFORMATION
Wheelchairs: Accommodated
Helpers: Admitted
Prices: Normal prices apply for the disabled and helpers
Disabled Toilets: Available
Contact: (02476) 314752   (Bookings are not necessary)

Travelling Supporters' Information:
Routes: Exit the M6 at Junction 3 and follow signs for the B4113. At the next roundabout, take the first exit and head north, passing underneath the M6 and continuing up Longford Road into Coventry Road. The entrance to the ground is on the right after passing the cemetery on the left. Take the 3rd exit at the mini-roundabout.

BIGGLESWADE TOWN FC

Founded: 1874
Former Names: Biggleswade FC
Nickname: 'The Waders'
Ground: The Carlsberg Stadium, Langford Road, Biggleswade SG18 9JT
Record Attendance: Approximately 2,000

Colours: Green & White striped shirts, Green shorts
Telephone Nº: (01767) 315547
Fax Number: (01767) 315547
Ground Capacity: 3,000
Seating Capacity: 300
Web Site: www.biggleswadetownfc.co.uk

GENERAL INFORMATION
Car Parking: At the ground
Coach Parking: At the ground
Nearest Railway Station: Biggleswade (½ mile)
Club Shop: At the ground
Opening Times: Matchdays only
Telephone Nº: –

GROUND INFORMATION
Away Supporters' Entrances & Sections:
No usual segregation

ADMISSION INFO (2011/2012 PRICES)
Adult Standing: £8.00
Adult Seating: £8.00
Concessionary Standing: £5.00
Concessionary Seating: £5.00
Note: Under-16s are admitted free of charge when accompanied by a paying adult
Programme Price: Included in admission prices

DISABLED INFORMATION
Wheelchairs: Accommodated
Helpers: Admitted
Prices: Normal prices apply for the disabled and helpers
Disabled Toilets: Available
Contact: (01767) 315547   (Bookings are not necessary)

Travelling Supporters' Information:
Routes: The Stadium is located just to the South of the A1 at Biggleswade. Exit the A1 at the northernmost roundabout by the Sainsbury's superstore and follow the A6001 (Hill Lane) into Biggleswade. Continue heading southwards along the A6001 into Shortmead Street then turn right at the mini-roundabout into St. Andrews Street. Continue along then turn right at the traffic lights shortly after the bend in the road onto Hitchin Street. Go straight on at the next two roundabouts, pass under the A1 and the entrance to the ground is on the right, after approximately 200 yards.

BURNHAM FC

Founded: 1878
Former Names: None
Nickname: 'The Blues'
Ground: The Gore, Wymers Wood Road, Burnham, Slough SL1 8JG
Record Attendance: 2,380 (2nd April 1983)

Colours: Blue & White quartered shirts with Blue shorts
Telephone N°: 07771 677337
Fax Number: (01628) 668654
Ground Capacity: 2,500
Seating Capacity: 300
Web Site: www.burnhamfc.com

GENERAL INFORMATION
Car Parking: At the ground
Coach Parking: At the ground
Nearest Railway Station: Taplow (1½ miles)
Club Shop: None
Opening Times: –
Telephone N°: –

GROUND INFORMATION
Away Supporters' Entrances & Sections:
No usual segregation

ADMISSION INFO (2011/2012 PRICES)
Adult Standing: £8.00
Adult Seating: £8.00
Concessionary Standing: £4.00
Concessionary Seating: £4.00
Under-16s Standing: £1.00
Under-16s Seating: £1.00
Programme Price: £1.50

DISABLED INFORMATION
Wheelchairs: Accommodated
Helpers: Admitted
Prices: Normal prices apply for the disabled and helpers
Disabled Toilets: Available
Contact: 07771 677337 (Bookings are not necessary)

Travelling Supporters' Information:
Routes: Exit the M4 at Junction 7 and turn left onto the A4 signposted for Maidenhead. After a short distance, turn right at the roundabout by Sainsbury's into Lent Rise Road and continue, passing under the railway line and going straight on at two roundabouts before forking right into Wymers Wood Road. The ground is on the right hand side of the road almost immediately.

CHALFONT ST. PETER FC

Founded: 1926
Former Names: None
Nickname: 'Saints'
Ground: Mill Meadow, Gravel Hill, Chalfont St. Peter, SL9 9QX
Record Attendance: 2,550 (during 1985)
Pitch Size: 109 × 70 yards

Colours: Red and Green shirts with Red shorts
Telephone Nº: (01753) 885797 (Clubhouse)
Fax Number: None
Ground Capacity: 2,500
Seating Capacity: 220
Web Site: www.chalfontstpeterafc.co.uk

GENERAL INFORMATION
Car Parking: At the ground
Coach Parking: At the ground
Nearest Railway Station: Gerrards Cross (1½ miles)
Nearest Bus Station: Chalfont St. Peter
Club Shop: At the ground
Opening Times: Matchdays only
Telephone Nº: 07153 885797

GROUND INFORMATION
Away Supporters' Entrances & Sections:
No usual segregation

ADMISSION INFO (2011/2012 PRICES)
Adult Standing: £8.00 ·
Adult Seating: £8.00
Senior Citizen/Junior Standing: £4.00
Senior Citizen/Junior Seating: £4.00
Programme Price: £1.00

DISABLED INFORMATION
Wheelchairs: Accommodated
Helpers: Admitted
Prices: Normal prices apply for the disabled and helpers
Disabled Toilets: None
Contact: (01753) 885797 (Bookings are not necessary)

Travelling Supporters' Information:
Routes: Exit the M40 at Junction 1 and take the A40 northwards past Denham onto the A413 Amersham Road. Pass underneath the M25 and head towards Chalfont St. Peter along the A413, going straight on at two roundabouts. Shortly after crossing the second roundabout, turn off left and follow the road to Mill Meadow.

CHERTSEY TOWN FC

Founded: 1890
Former Names: None
Nickname: 'The Curfews'
Ground: Alwyns Lane, Chertsey   KT16 9DW
Record Attendance: 2,150 (4th December 1993)
Pitch Size: 110 × 72 yards

Colours: White shirts and shorts
Telephone N°: (01932) 561744
Fax Number: None
Ground Capacity: 3,000
Seating Capacity: 240
Web Site: www.chertseytown-fc.co.uk

GENERAL INFORMATION
Car Parking: Limited number of spaces at the ground
Coach Parking: At the ground
Nearest Railway Station: Chertsey (½ mile)
Nearest Bus Station: Chertsey
Club Shop: None, but a limited selection of CTFC items are available at the ground on matchdays
Opening Times: –
Telephone N°: –

GROUND INFORMATION
Away Supporters' Entrances & Sections:
No usual segregation

ADMISSION INFO (2011/2012 PRICES)
Adult Standing: £8.00
Adult Seating: £8.00
Senior Citizen/Junior/Concessionary Standing: £4.00
Senior Citizen/Junior/Concessionary Seating: £4.00
Programme Price: £1.50

DISABLED INFORMATION
Wheelchairs: Accommodated
Helpers: Admitted
Prices: £4.00 for the disabled. Helpers are admitted free
Disabled Toilets: Available in the clubhouse
Contact: (01932) 561744   (Bookings are not necessary)

Travelling Supporters' Information:
Routes: Exit the M25 at Junction 11 and take the A317 (St. Peter's Way) towards Chertsey. Take the first exit at the roundabout into Chertsey Road then continue straight on into Fordwater Road (B387) which then becomes Weir Road. At the T-junction at the bottom of Weir Road, turn left into Bridge Road (B375), continue along as the road sweeps left then bears left into London Street. Take the second exit at the mini-roundabout (with the shopping centre on the left) and continue into Windsor Street, turning left into Alwyns Lane shortly after the road bends right. The ground is on the left, a short way along Alwyns Lane.

DAVENTRY TOWN FC

Founded: 1886
Former Names: None
Nickname: 'Town'
Ground: Communications Park, Browns Road, Daventry NN11 4NS
Record Attendance: 850 (1989)

Colours: Violet shirts and shorts
Telephone Nº: (01327) 311239
Fax Number: 0844 846-8199
Ground Capacity: 2,000
Seating Capacity: 250
Web Site: www.dtfc.co.uk

GENERAL INFORMATION
Car Parking: At the ground
Coach Parking: At the ground
Nearest Railway Station: Long Buckby (6 miles)
Club Shop: None
Opening Times: –
Telephone Nº: –

GROUND INFORMATION
Away Supporters' Entrances & Sections: No usual segregation

ADMISSION INFO (2011/2012 PRICES)
Adult Standing: £9.00
Adult Seating: £9.00
Concessionary Standing: £5.00
Concessionary Seating: £5.00
Under-16s Standing/Seating: £1.00
Programme Price: £1.00

DISABLED INFORMATION
Wheelchairs: Accommodated
Helpers: Admitted
Prices: Normal prices apply for the disabled and helpers
Disabled Toilets: –
Contact: (01327) 311239   (Bookings are not necessary)

Travelling Supporters' Information:
Routes: Take the A45 to the western outskirts of Daventry near to Staverton Park Golf Club and, at the roundabout junction with the A425, cross over into Browns Road. The ground is on the left hand side of the road after approximately 200 yards.

FLEET TOWN FC

Founded: 1890 (Re-formed in 1947)
Former Names: Fleet FC
Nickname: 'The Blues'
Ground: Calthorpe Park, Crookham Road, Fleet, GU51 5FA
Record Attendance: 1,336 (9th January 2005)

Colours: Sky Blue shirts with Navy Blue shorts
Telephone N°: (01252) 623804
Fax Number: (01252) 648749
Ground Capacity: 2,000
Seating Capacity: 200
Web Site: www.fleettownfc.co.uk

GENERAL INFORMATION
Car Parking: At the ground
Coach Parking: At the ground
Nearest Railway Station: Fleet (1½ miles)
Club Shop: At the ground
Opening Times: Matchdays only
Telephone N°: –

GROUND INFORMATION
Away Supporters' Entrances & Sections:
No usual segregation

ADMISSION INFO (2011/2012 PRICES)
Adult Standing/Seating: £8.00
Senior Citizen Standing/Seating: £4.00
Under-16s Standing/Seating: £4.00
Under-12s Standing/Seating: Free of charge
Programme Price: £1.50

DISABLED INFORMATION
Wheelchairs: Accommodated
Helpers: Admitted
Prices: Normal prices apply for the disabled and helpers
Disabled Toilets: Available
Contact: (01252) 623804 (Bookings are necessary)

Travelling Supporters' Information:
Routes: Exit the M3 at Junction 4A and follow signs for Fleet taking the A327 southwards before joining the A3013 Fleet Road. Continue along this road passing through Fleet and, at The Oat Sheaf Pub crossroads (at the junction with the A323), continue straight ahead into Crookham Road. The ground is down the hill on the right-hand side after about 300 yards.

LEIGHTON TOWN FC

Founded: 1885
Former Names: Leighton United FC
Nickname: 'Reds'
Ground: Bell Close, Lake Street, Leighton Buzzard, LU7 1RX
Record Attendance: 1,522 (30th January 1993)

Colours: Red and White striped shirts with Red shorts
Telephone Nº: (01525) 373311
Ground Capacity: 2,800
Seating Capacity: 155
Web Site: www.leightontownfc.co.uk

GENERAL INFORMATION
Car Parking: At the ground
Coach Parking: At the ground
Nearest Railway Station: Leighton Buzzard (1 mile)
Club Shop: None
Opening Times: –
Telephone Nº: –

GROUND INFORMATION
Away Supporters' Entrances & Sections:
No usual segregation

ADMISSION INFO (2011/2012 PRICES)
Adult Standing/Seating: £8.00
Concessionary Standing/Seating: £5.00
Child Standing/Seating: £2.00
Programme Price: £1.50

DISABLED INFORMATION
Wheelchairs: Accommodated
Helpers: Admitted
Prices: Normal prices apply for the disabled and helpers
Disabled Toilets: None
Contact: (01525) 373311 (Bookings are not necessary)

Travelling Supporters' Information:
Routes: The ground is located by the side of the A4146 Leighton Buzzard to Hemel Hempstead road, approximately ¼ mile south of Leighton Town Centre. The entrance to the ground is located directly opposite the Morrison's Supermarket Petrol Station.

MARLOW FC

Founded: 1870
Former Names: Great Marlow FC
Nickname: 'The Blues'
Ground: Alfred Davies Memorial Ground, Oak Tree Road, Marlow SL7 3ED
Record Attendance: 3,000 (1994)

Colours: Royal Blue shirts and shorts
Telephone N°: (01628) 483970
Fax Number: (01628) 477032
Ground Capacity: 3,000
Seating Capacity: 250
Web Site: www.marlowfc.co.uk

GENERAL INFORMATION
Car Parking: At the ground
Coach Parking: At the ground
Nearest Railway Station: Marlow (¾ mile)
Club Shop: None
Opening Times: –
Telephone N°: –

GROUND INFORMATION
Away Supporters' Entrances & Sections:
No usual segregation

ADMISSION INFO (2011/2012 PRICES)
Adult Standing: £8.00
Adult Seating: £8.00
Senior Citizen/Junior Standing: £4.00
Senior Citizen/Junior Seating: £4.00
Programme Price: £1.00

DISABLED INFORMATION
Wheelchairs: Accommodated
Helpers: Admitted
Prices: Normal prices apply for the disabled. Helpers are admitted free of charge
Disabled Toilets: None
Contact: (01628) 483970 (Bookings are necessary)

Travelling Supporters' Information:
Routes: Exit the M40 at Junction 4 and take the A404 towards Marlow. Take the first exit for the A4155, follow the A4155 towards Marlow and turn right immediately after the Esso service station called 'On The Run' into Maple Rise. Cross directly over the crossroads into Oak Tree Road and the ground can be found approximately on the left after approximately 100 yards.

NORTH GREENFORD UNITED FC

Founded: 1944
Former Names: None
Nickname: 'The Blues'
Ground: Berkeley Fields, Berkeley Avenue, Greenford UB6 0NX
Record Attendance: 985
Colours: Blue and White shirts with Blue shorts
Telephone Nº: (020) 8422-8923
Ground Capacity: 2,000
Seating Capacity: 150
Web Site: www.northgreenfordunitedfc.co.uk

GENERAL INFORMATION
Car Parking: At the ground
Coach Parking: At the ground
Nearest Railway Station: Greenford (½ mile)
Nearest Tube Station: Greenford (½ mile)
Club Shop: None
Opening Times: –
Telephone Nº: –

GROUND INFORMATION
Away Supporters' Entrances & Sections:
No usual segregation

ADMISSION INFO (2011/2012 PRICES)
Adult Standing: £8.00
Adult Seating: £8.00
Senior Citizen/Junior Standing: £4.00
Senior Citizen/Junior Seating: £4.00
Programme Price: Included with admission

DISABLED INFORMATION
Wheelchairs: Accommodated
Helpers: Admitted
Prices: Concessionary prices are charged for the disabled and helpers
Disabled Toilets: Available
Contact: (020) 8422-8923 (Bookings are necessary)

Travelling Supporters' Information:
Routes: Exit the M25 at Junction 16 and take the M40 towards London. Continue into the A40 then exit at the Greenford Roundabout onto the A4127 heading into Greenford. Pass under the railway bridge and continue northwards along Greenford Road passing the Paradise Fields Shopping Complex. Turn right into Berkeley Avenue at the traffic lights opposite Glaxo and the entrance to the ground is at the bottom of the hill on the right.

NORTHWOOD FC

Founded: 1899
Former Names: None
Nickname: 'Woods'
Ground: Northwood Park, Chestnut Avenue, Northwood   HA6 1HR
Record Attendance: 1,642 (vs Chelsea, 1997)
Pitch Size: 118 × 80 yards
Colours: Red shirts and shorts
Telephone Nº: (01923) 827148
Ground Capacity: 3,075
Seating Capacity: 308
Web site: www.northwoodfc.com

GENERAL INFORMATION
Car Parking: 100 spaces available at the ground
Coach Parking: In Chestnut Avenue
Nearest Underground Station: Northwood Hills (½ mile)
Club Shop: At the ground
Opening Times: Matchdays only
Telephone Nº: None

GROUND INFORMATION
Away Supporters' Entrances & Sections:
No usual segregation

ADMISSION INFO (2011/2012 PRICES)
Adult Standing/Seating: £8.00
Concessionary Standing/Seating: £4.00
Under-16s Standing/Seating: Free of charge
Programme Price: £1.50

DISABLED INFORMATION
Wheelchairs: Accommodated
Helpers: Admitted
Prices: Normal prices apply
Disabled Toilets: None
Contact: (01923) 827148   (Bookings are not necessary)

Travelling Supporters' Information:
Routes: The ground is situated just off the Pinner to Rickmansworth road (A404) in Northwood. Approaching from Pinner turn left into Chestnut Avenue by the large grey railway bridge for the ground.

RUGBY TOWN FC

Founded: 1956
Former Names: Glebe Rangers FC, New Bilton Juniors FC, Valley Sports FC, Valley Sports Rugby FC, V.S. Rugby FC and Rugby United FC
Nickname: 'The Valley'
Ground: Butlin Road, Rugby CV21 3SD
Record Attendance: 3,961 (1984)
Pitch Size: 110 × 72 yards
Colours: Sky Blue shirts with White shorts
Contact Telephone Nº: 07976 284614
Correspondence: Melbros House, Great Central Way, Rugby CV21 3XH
Ground Capacity: 6,000
Seating Capacity: 740
Web site: www.rugbytownfc.com

GENERAL INFORMATION
Car Parking: At the ground
Coach Parking: At the ground
Nearest Railway Station: Rugby (1 mile)
Nearest Bus Station: Rugby
Club Shop: At the ground
Opening Times: Matchdays only
Telephone Nº: (01788) 844806

GROUND INFORMATION
Away Supporters' Entrances & Sections:
No usual segregation

ADMISSION INFO (2011/2012 PRICES)
Adult Standing: £8.00
Adult Seating: £8.00
Senior Citizen/Junior Standing: £4.00
Senior Citizen/Junior Seating: £4.00
Programme Price: £2.00

DISABLED INFORMATION
Wheelchairs: Accommodated
Helpers: Admitted
Prices: Normal prices apply
Disabled Toilets: Available
Contact: 07976 284614

Travelling Supporters' Information:
Routes: Exit the M6 at Junction 1 and take the A426 into Rugby. Cross the railway and turn left from Newbold Road into Wood Street. Take the second turning on the right into Railway Terrace then turn left at the end along the B5414 Clifton Road. Butlin Road is about ½ mile along, near the Golf Course.

SLOUGH TOWN FC

Slough Town FC are groundsharing with Beaconsfield SYCOB FC during the 2011-2012 season.

Founded: 1890
Former Names: Slough FC and Slough United FC
Nickname: 'The Rebels'
Ground: Holloways Park, Windsor Road, Beaconsfield HP9 2SE
Record Attendance: 8,000

Colours: Amber shirts with Navy Blue shorts
Contact Telephone Nº: 07989 434371
Ground Capacity: 3,500
Seating Capacity: 200
Web site: www.sloughtownfc.net
E-mail: secretary@sloughtownfc.net

GENERAL INFORMATION
Car Parking: At the ground
Coach Parking: At the ground
Nearest Railway Station: Beaconsfield (2½ miles)
Club Shop: None
Opening Times: –
Telephone Nº: –

GROUND INFORMATION
Away Supporters' Entrances & Sections:
No usual segregation

ADMISSION INFO (2011/2012 PRICES)
Adult Standing: £8.00
Adult Seating: £8.00
Child/Senior Citizen Standing: £4.00
Child/Senior Citizen Seating: £4.00
Programme Price: £1.50

DISABLED INFORMATION
Wheelchairs: Accommodated
Helpers: Admitted
Prices: Normal prices apply for the disabled and helpers
Disabled Toilets: Available
Contact: 07989 434371 (Bookings are not necessary)

Travelling Supporters' Information:
Routes: Exit the M40 at Junction 2 and head into the Beaconsfield Motorway Service area. In the services, follow the signs for Beaconsfield SYCOB, crossing the A355 and heading back towards the M40. After approximately 150 yards turn left into the ground and the car park and Clubhouse are on the right after 200 yards.

ST. NEOTS TOWN FC

Unfortunately, no ground photograph for St. Neots Town FC was available at the time of going to press.

Founded: 1879
Former Names: St. Neots FC, St. Neots & District FC
Nickname: 'The Saints'
Ground: The Hunts Post Community Stadium, Kesterway, St. Neots PE19 6SN
Record Attendance: 2,000 (during 1966)
Pitch Size: 110 × 72 yards
Colours: Sky Blue shirts with Navy Blue shorts & socks
Telephone Nº: (01480) 470012
Ground Capacity: 3,000
Seating Capacity: 250
Web Site: www.stneotsfc.com

GENERAL INFORMATION
Car Parking: Limited spaces at the ground but further spaces are available in a nearby School Car Park
Coach Parking: At the ground
Nearest Railway Station: St. Neots (¼ mile)
Nearest Bus Station: St. Neots
Club Shop: At the ground
Opening Times: Matchdays only
Telephone Nº: –

GROUND INFORMATION
Away Supporters' Entrances & Sections: No usual segregation

ADMISSION INFO (2011/2012 PRICES)
Adult Standing: £8.00
Adult Seating: £8.00
Senior Citizen Standing/Seating: £5.00
Under-17s Standing/Seating: £3.00
Note: Under-11s are admitted free with a paying adult
Programme Price: £2.00

DISABLED INFORMATION
Wheelchairs: Accommodated
Helpers: Admitted
Prices: Normal prices apply for the disabled and helpers
Disabled Toilets: Available
Contact: (01480) 470012   (Bookings are necessary)

Travelling Supporters' Information:
Routes: Exit the A1 onto the A428 at St. Neots. Continue along the A428 passing Tesco and take the first exit at the next roundabout onto the B1428 (Cambridge Road). Follow this road towards St. Neots town centre, turn right at the roundabout just before the railway bridge and the ground is in the top left hand corner of the housing estate, beside the railway.

UXBRIDGE FC

Founded: 1871
Former Names: Uxbridge Town FC
Nickname: 'The Reds'
Ground: Honeycroft, Horton Road, West Drayton, UB7 8HX
Record Attendance: 1,000 (1981)

Colours: Red shirts with White shorts
Telephone N°: (01895) 443557
Fax Number: (01895) 445830
Ground Capacity: 3,770
Seating Capacity: 339
Web Site: www.uxbridgefc.co.uk

GENERAL INFORMATION
Car Parking: At the ground and also street parking
Coach Parking: At the ground
Nearest Railway Station: West Drayton (½ mile)
Nearest Tube Station: Uxbridge (3 miles)
Club Shop: None
Opening Times: –
Telephone N°: –

GROUND INFORMATION
Away Supporters' Entrances & Sections:
No usual segregation

ADMISSION INFO (2011/2012 PRICES)
Adult Standing: £8.00
Adult Seating: £8.00
Senior Citizen/Junior Standing: £4.00
Senior Citizen/Junior Seating: £4.00
Programme Price: £1.50

DISABLED INFORMATION
Wheelchairs: Accommodated (2 spaces available only)
Helpers: Admitted
Prices: Normal prices apply for the disabled. Helpers are admitted free of charge
Disabled Toilets: Available
Contact: (01895) 445830 (Bookings are necessary)

Travelling Supporters' Information:
Routes: Exit the M4 at Junction 4 and follow the A408 northwards. After passing Heathpark Golf Course and crossing the railway line and the canal, take the slip road before the flyover onto Horton Road. Take the second exit at Stockley Park Roundabout continuing on Horton Road and entrance to the ground is on the right after a short distance, just before the bend in the road.

WOODFORD UNITED FC

Founded: 1946
Former Names: None
Nickname: 'The Reds'
Ground: Byfield Road, Woodford Halse, Daventry, NN11 3TR
Record Attendance: 1,500

Colours: Red shirts and shorts
Telephone N°: (01327) 263734
Fax Number: (01327) 263734
Ground Capacity: 3,000
Seating Capacity: 252
Web Site: www.woodford-united.co.uk

GENERAL INFORMATION
Car Parking: At the ground
Coach Parking: At the ground
Nearest Railway Station: Banbury (12 miles)
Club Shop: None
Opening Times: –
Telephone N°: –

GROUND INFORMATION
Away Supporters' Entrances & Sections:
No usual segregation

ADMISSION INFO (2011/2012 PRICES)
Adult Standing: £8.00
Adult Seating: £8.00
Senior Citizen/Junior Standing: £4.00
Senior Citizen/Junior Seating: £4.00
Programme Price: £1.50

DISABLED INFORMATION
Wheelchairs: Accommodated
Helpers: Admitted
Prices: Concessionary prices are charged for the disabled and helpers
Disabled Toilets: Available
Contact: (01327) 263734   (Bookings are not necessary)

Travelling Supporters' Information:
Routes: Take the A361 south from Daventry or north from Banbury and head to Byfield village. At the dual mini-roundabouts in Byfield, turn off the A361 and head east towards Hinton along Woodford Road into Byfield Road. Continue along Byfield Road, passing through Hinton and the ground is on the left hand side of the road just after passing the Industrial Estate.

The Evo-Stik League Southern Division One South & West

Secretary Jason Mills

Correspondence
secretary@southern-football-league.co.uk

Web Site www.southern-football-league.co.uk

Clubs for the 2011/2012 Season

Abingdon United FC	Page 53
Bideford FC	Page 54
Bishop's Cleeve FC	Page 55
Bridgwater Town FC	Page 56
Cinderford Town FC	Page 57
Clevedon Town FC	Page 58
Didcot Town FC	Page 59
Gosport Borough FC	Page 60
Halesowen Town FC	Page 61
Hungerford Town FC	Page 62
Mangotsfield United FC	Page 63
North Leigh FC	Page 64
Paulton Rovers FC	Page 65
Poole Town FC	Page 66
Sholing FC	Page 67
Stourport Swifts FC	Page 68
Taunton Town FC	Page 69
Thatcham Town FC	Page 70
Tiverton Town FC	Page 71
Wimborne Town FC	Page 72
Yate Town FC	Page 73

ABINGDON UNITED FC

Founded: 1946
Former Names: None
Nickname: 'The Us'
Ground: The North Court, North Court Road, Abingdon OX14 1PL
Record Attendance: 2,000 (vs Oxford United – 2002)

Colours: Yellow shirts and shorts
Telephone Nº: (01235) 203203
Fax Number: (01235) 202124
Ground Capacity: 2,000
Seating Capacity: 158
Web Site: www.abingdonunitedfc.co.uk

GENERAL INFORMATION
Car Parking: At the ground
Coach Parking: At the ground
Nearest Railway Station: Radley (2¼ miles)
Club Shop: None
Opening Times: –
Telephone Nº: –

GROUND INFORMATION
Away Supporters' Entrances & Sections:
No usual segregation

ADMISSION INFO (2011/2012 PRICES)
Adult Standing: £6.00
Adult Seating: £6.00
Senior Citizen/Under-16s Standing: £2.50
Senior Citizen/Under-16s Seating: £2.50
Programme Price: £1.50

DISABLED INFORMATION
Wheelchairs: Accommodated
Helpers: Admitted
Prices: Normal prices apply for the disabled and helpers
Disabled Toilets: Available
Contact: (01235) 203203   (Bookings are not necessary)

Travelling Supporters' Information:
Routes: Take the A34 southwards from Oxford and exit onto the A4183 just to the north of Abingdon. Continue into Abingdon along the A4183 (Oxford Road), go straight on at the roundabout then take the 6th turning on the right into Northcourt Road. The entrance to the ground is then immediately on the left.

BIDEFORD FC

Founded: 1949
Former Names: Bideford Town FC
Nickname: 'The Robins'
Ground: The Sports Ground, Kingsley Road, Bideford EX39 2NG
Record Attendance: 6,000

Colours: Red shirts and shorts
Telephone Nº: (01237) 474974
Ground Capacity: 6,000
Seating Capacity: 375
Web Site: www.bidefordafc.co.uk

GENERAL INFORMATION
Car Parking: At the ground
Coach Parking: In Kingsley Road
Nearest Railway Station: Barnstaple (9½ miles)
Club Shop: At the ground
Opening Times: Matchdays only from 2.00pm to kick-off
Telephone Nº: –

GROUND INFORMATION
Away Supporters' Entrances & Sections:
No usual segregation

ADMISSION INFO (2011/2012 PRICES)
Adult Standing: £8.00
Adult Seating: £8.00
Senior Citizen/Junior Standing: £5.00
Senior Citizen/Junior Seating: £5.00
Programme Price: £1.50

DISABLED INFORMATION
Wheelchairs: Accommodated
Helpers: Admitted
Prices: Normal prices apply for the disabled and helpers
Disabled Toilets: Available
Contact: (01237) 474974 (Bookings are necessary)

Travelling Supporters' Information:
Routes: Take the A39 over the high level Torridge Bridge then turn left at the roundabout towards Bideford along Kingsley Road. Follow this road down towards the River Quayside and the ground is on the right hand side across the road from the Morrisons Supermarket.

BISHOP'S CLEEVE FC

Founded: 1905
Former Names: None
Nickname: 'The Villagers'
Ground: Kayte Lane, Bishop's Cleeve, Cheltenham, GL52 3PD
Record Attendance: 1,300 (vs Newport County in July 2006)

Colours: Blue shirts and shorts
Telephone Nº: (01242) 676166
Fax Number: (01386) 750227
Ground Capacity: 1,500
Seating Capacity: 50
Web Site: www.bishopscleevefc.com

GENERAL INFORMATION
Car Parking: At the ground
Coach Parking: Inside the ground
Nearest Railway Station: Cheltenham Spa (4 miles)
Club Shop: At the ground
Opening Times: –
Telephone Nº: –

GROUND INFORMATION
Away Supporters' Entrances & Sections:
No usual segregation

ADMISSION INFO (2011/2012 PRICES)
Adult Standing: £6.00
Adult Seating: £6.00
Senior Citizen/Junior Standing: £4.00
Senior Citizen/Junior Seating: £4.00
Programme Price: £1.00

DISABLED INFORMATION
Wheelchairs: Accommodated
Helpers: Admitted
Prices: Concessionary prices are charged for the disabled and helpers
Disabled Toilets: Available
Contact: (01242) 676166 (Bookings are not necessary)

Travelling Supporters' Information:
Routes: The ground is situated off the A435 Cheltenham to Bishop's Cleeve road just to the south of Bishop's Cleeve. Head north on the A435 from Cheltenham passing the Racecourse then take the first turn on the right into Southam Lane. Take the next left into Kayte Lane and the ground is on the left after approximately 500 yards.

BRIDGWATER TOWN FC 1984

Founded: 1898 (Re-formed several times since)
Former Names: Bridgwater Town FC
Nickname: 'The Robins'
Ground: Fairfax Park, College Way, Bath Road, Bridgwater TA6 4TZ
Record Attendance: 1,112 (26th February 1997)
Colours: Red shirts with White shorts
Telephone Nº: (01278) 446899
Fax Number: (01278) 446899
Ground Capacity: 2,500
Seating Capacity: 318
Web Site: www.bridgwatertownfc1984.co.uk

GENERAL INFORMATION
Car Parking: 150 spaces available at the ground
Coach Parking: At the ground
Nearest Railway Station: Bridgwater (¾ mile)
Club Shop: At the ground
Opening Times: Matchdays only
Telephone Nº: 07849 510210

GROUND INFORMATION
Away Supporters' Entrances & Sections:
No usual segregation

ADMISSION INFO (2011/2012 PRICES)
Adult Standing: £8.00
Adult Seating: £8.00
Senior Citizen Standing: £6.00
Senior Citizen Seating: £6.00
Under-16s Standing/Seating: £2.00
Programme Price: £1.50

DISABLED INFORMATION
Wheelchairs: Accommodated
Helpers: Admitted
Prices: Normal prices apply for the disabled. Helpers are admitted free of charge
Disabled Toilets: Available
Contact: (01278) 446899 (Bookings are preferred)

Travelling Supporters' Information:
Routes: Exit the M5 at Junction 23 and turn left onto the A39 heading towards Glastonbury. Continue over the hill until the junction just past Knowle Hall (on the left). Turn right towards Bridgwater (A39), pass over the motorway and continue along Bath Road. Pass the old Innova factory on the right and slow down as the road narrows with terraced houses on both sides. Take the turning immediately on the left (signposted Bridgwater College) by the Bridgwater & Albion RFC Ground, just before crossing the railway bridge. In College Way, take the second turning on the right into the ground just before the College gates.

CINDERFORD TOWN FC

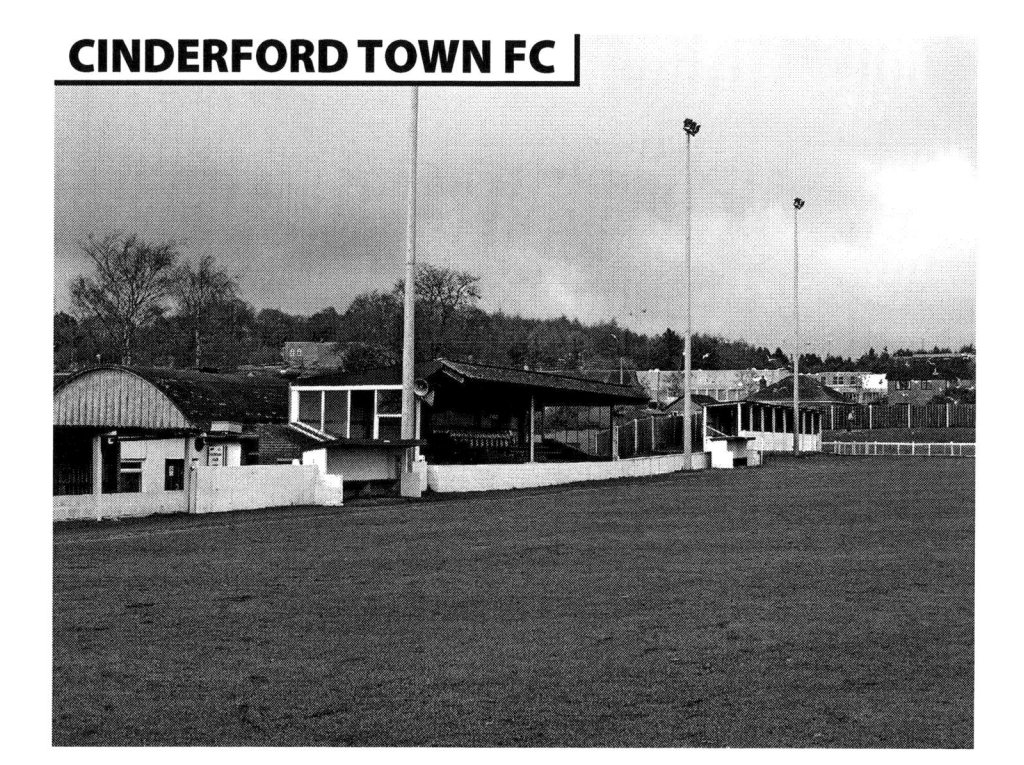

Founded: 1922
Former Names: None
Nickname: 'The Foresters'
Ground: The Causeway, Edge Hills Road, Cinderford, GL14 2QH
Record Attendance: 4,850 (1955/56 season)

Colours: Black and White striped shirts, Black shorts
Telephone Nº: (01594) 827147
Fax Number: (01594) 835945
Ground Capacity: 3,500
Seating Capacity: 250
Web Site: www.pitchero.com/clubs/cinderfordtown

GENERAL INFORMATION
Car Parking: At the ground
Coach Parking: At the ground
Nearest Railway Station: Lydney (11½ miles)
Club Shop: At the ground
Opening Times: Matchdays only
Telephone Nº: –

GROUND INFORMATION
Away Supporters' Entrances & Sections:
No usual segregation

ADMISSION INFO (2011/2012 PRICES)
Adult Standing: £8.00
Adult Seating: £8.00
Senior Citizen/Concessionary Standing: £4.00
Senior Citizen/Concessionary Seating: £4.00
Under-14s Standing/Seating: £2.00
Programme Price: £1.00

DISABLED INFORMATION
Wheelchairs: Accommodated
Helpers: Admitted
Prices: Normal prices apply for the disabled and helpers
Disabled Toilets: None
Contact: (01594) 827147   (Bookings are not necessary)

Travelling Supporters' Information:
Routes: Take the A48 southwards from Gloucester to Elton and join the A4151. Pass through Littledean then turn right into the High Street and continue along as the road becomes 'The Ruffitt' following it into Cinderford. At the junction turn into Causeway Road and Edge Hills Road is the 2nd turning on the left. The entrance to the ground is then on the left after the bend in the road.

CLEVEDON TOWN FC

Founded: 1880
Former Names: None
Nickname: 'The Seasiders'
Ground: Hand Stadium, Davis Lane, Clevedon, BS21 6TG
Record Attendance: 3,264
Pitch Size: 100 × 70 yards

Colours: Blue and White striped shirts, Blue shorts
Telephone Nº: (01275) 871600
Office Phone Nº: (01275) 871601
Fax Number: (01275) 871601
Ground Capacity: 3,650
Seating Capacity: 300
Web site: www.pitchero.com/clubs/clevedontown

GENERAL INFORMATION
Car Parking: 240 spaces available at the ground
Coach Parking: 6 spaces available at the ground
Nearest Railway Station: Yatton
Nearest Bus Station: Bristol
Club Shop: At the ground
Opening Times: Matchdays only
Telephone Nº: (01275) 871601

GROUND INFORMATION
Away Supporters' Entrances:
No usual segregation

ADMISSION INFO (2011/2012 PRICES)
Adult Standing: £8.00
Adult Seating: £8.00
Child Standing: £1.00
Child Seating: £1.00
Senior Citizen Standing: £5.00
Senior Citizen Seating: £5.00
Programme Price: £1.50

DISABLED INFORMATION
Wheelchairs: Accommodated
Helpers: Admitted
Prices: Normal prices apply
Disabled Toilets: Available
Contact: (01275) 871600   (Bookings are not necessary)

Travelling Supporters' Information:
Routes: Exit the M5 at Junction 20 and follow signs for The Hand Stadium. Take the 1st left into Central Way (at the traffic island just after the motorway), take 1st left at the mini-roundabout into Kenn Road then 2nd left into Davis Lane. The ground is ½ mile on the right; From Bristol: Take the B3130 to Clevedon then turn left into Court Lane (opposite Clevedon Court) then turn right after 1 mile and the ground is on the left.

DIDCOT TOWN FC

Founded: 1907
Former Names: None
Nickname: 'Railwaymen'
Ground: NPower Loop Meadow Stadium, Bowmont Water, Didcot OX11 7GA
Record Attendance: 1,512 (2005)

Colours: Red and White shirts with White shorts
Telephone Nº: (01235) 813138
Fax Number: (01235) 816352
Ground Capacity: 5,000
Seating Capacity: 250
Web Site: www.didcottownfc.com

GENERAL INFORMATION
Car Parking: At the ground
Coach Parking: At the ground
Nearest Railway Station: Didcot Parkway (5 minute walk)
Club Shop: At the ground
Opening Times: Matchdays only
Telephone Nº: –

GROUND INFORMATION
Away Supporters' Entrances & Sections:
No usual segregation

ADMISSION INFO (2011/2012 PRICES)
Adult Standing: £9.00
Adult Seating: £9.00
Concessionary Standing/Seating: £5.00
Under-16s Standing/Seating: £2.00
Note: Under-16s are admitted free when accompanied by a paying adult.
Programme Price: £2.00

DISABLED INFORMATION
Wheelchairs: Accommodated
Helpers: Admitted
Prices: Normal prices apply for the disabled and helpers
Disabled Toilets: Available
Contact: (01235) 813138   (Bookings are not necessary)

Travelling Supporters' Information:
Routes: From the A34 take the A4130 towards Didcot passing the Power Station on your left. Take the first exit at the first roundabout, the 3rd exit at the next roundabout then go straight on at the next two roundabouts. After crossing the railwayline turn right at the next roundabout into Avon Way. Go over the speed bump go straight over the next roundabout into Bowmont Water. The Ground and car park is on the left.

GOSPORT BOROUGH FC

Founded: 1944
Former Names: Gosport Borough Athletic FC
Nickname: 'The Boro'
Ground: GHS Stadium, Privett Park, Privett Road, Gosport PO12 3SX
Record Attendance: 4,770 (1951)

Colours: Yellow shirts with Navy Blue shorts
Telephone Nº: (023) 9250-1042
Fax Number: (01329) 235961
Ground Capacity: 4,500
Seating Capacity: 450
Web Site: www.gosportboroughfc.com

GENERAL INFORMATION
Car Parking: At the ground
Coach Parking: At the ground
Nearest Railway Station: Fareham (5½ miles)
Club Shop: At the ground
Opening Times: Matchdays only
Telephone Nº: –

GROUND INFORMATION
Away Supporters' Entrances & Sections:
No usual segregation

ADMISSION INFO (2011/2012 PRICES)
Adult Standing: £8.00
Adult Seating: £8.00
Concessionary Standing: £4.00
Concessionary Seating: £4.00
Note: Under-12s are admitted free of charge when accompanied by a paying adult
Programme Price: £1.50

DISABLED INFORMATION
Wheelchairs: Accommodated
Helpers: Admitted
Prices: Normal prices apply for the disabled and helpers
Disabled Toilets: Available
Contact: (023) 9250-1042   (Bookings are not necessary)

Travelling Supporters' Information:
Routes: Exit the M27 at Junction 11 and follow take the A27 Eastern Way towards Gosport. Turn left at the roundabout to join the A32 Gosport Road and head south into Gosport. Continue along the A32 as it becomes Fareham Road then, at the second roundabout in a junction with two roundabouts, take the 3rd exit (signposted Alverstoke, Stokes Bay, Privett Park) into Military Road. Continue straight down this road, pass the playing fields on the left, then turn left at the roundabout into Privett Road. The entrance to the ground is the 4th turning on the left, just after the junction with Privett Place.

HALESOWEN TOWN FC

Founded: 1873
Former Names: None
Nickname: 'The Yeltz'
Ground: The Grove, Old Hawne Lane, Halesowen, West Midlands B63 3TB
Record Attendance: 5,000 (19th November 1955)
Pitch Size: 110 × 70 yards
Colours: Shirts are Blue with White trim, White shorts
Telephone Nº: (0121) 661-9392
Fax Number: (0121) 314-5321
Ground Capacity: 3,150
Seating Capacity: 525
Web site: www.halesowentownfc.co.uk

GENERAL INFORMATION

Car Parking: 20 spaces available at the Social Club.
Coach Parking: Available near to the ground
Nearest Railway Station: Old Hill (2 miles)
Nearest Bus Station: Halesowen Town Centre
Club Shop: At the ground
Opening Times: Matchdays only
Telephone Nº: –

GROUND INFORMATION

Away Supporters' Entrances & Sections:
No usual segregation

ADMISSION INFO (2011/2012 PRICES)

Adult Standing/Seating: £8.00
Concessionary Standing/Seating: £5.00
Child Standing/Seating: £2.00 (When accompanied by a paying adult)
Programme Price: £1.50

DISABLED INFORMATION

Wheelchairs: 5 spaces available in total situated at the side of the Main Seating Stand
Helpers: Admitted
Prices: Free of charge for the disabled
Disabled Toilets: Available near the Main Stand
Contact: (0121) 661-9392 (Bookings are not necessary)

Travelling Supporters' Information:
Routes: Exit the M5 at Junction 3 and follow the A456 towards Kidderminster. At the first roundabout, turn right onto the A458 towards Dudley. Turn left at the next roundabout and follow signposts onto the A458 towards Stourbridge. Take the 3rd exit at the next roundabout and the ground is on the left hand side after approximately 400 yards.

HUNGERFORD TOWN FC

Founded: 1886
Former Names: None
Nickname: 'The Crusaders'
Ground: Town Ground, Bulpit Lane, Hungerford, RG17 0AY
Record Attendance: 1,684 (1988/89 season)

Colours: White shirts with White shorts
Contact Telephone Nº: 0782 502-1669
Ground Capacity: 2,500
Seating Capacity: 250
Web Site: www.hungerfordtownfootballclub.co.uk

GENERAL INFORMATION
Car Parking: At the ground
Coach Parking: At the ground
Nearest Railway Station: Hungerford (½ mile)
Club Shop: At the ground
Opening Times: Monday to Friday 6.30pm to 11.00pm and Saturday from 12.00pm to midnight
Telephone Nº: –

GROUND INFORMATION
Away Supporters' Entrances & Sections:
No usual segregation

ADMISSION INFO (2011/2012 PRICES)
Adult Standing: £8.00
Adult Seating: £8.00
Senior Citizen/Junior Standing: £4.50
Senior Citizen/Junior Seating: £4.50
Programme Price: £1.00

DISABLED INFORMATION
Wheelchairs: Accommodated
Helpers: Admitted
Prices: £4.50 for the disabled and helpers
Disabled Toilets: Available
Contact: 0782 502-1669 (Bookings are not necessary)

Travelling Supporters' Information:
Routes: Exit the M4 at Junction 14 and take the A338 towards Hungerford. Upon reaching Hungerford, turn right at the roundabout onto the A4 Bath Road, turn left at the next rounabout into Charnham Street then turn left again into Bridge Street (A338). The road becomes the High Street and pass under the railway line, carry straight on over three mini-roundabouts then take the next left into Priory Road. Continue to the end of the street and continue left into Priory Road then take the 3rd turning on the left into Bulpit Lane. The entrance to the ground is on the left shortly after crossing the junction with Priory Avenue.

MANGOTSFIELD UNITED FC

Founded: 1888 (Reformed 1951)
Former Names: Mangotsfield FC
Nickname: 'The Field'
Ground: Cossham Street, Mangotsfield, Bristol, BS16 9EN
Record Attendance: 2,386 (vs Bath City 1977-78)

Colours: Sky Blue shirts with Maroon shorts
Telephone Nº: (0117) 956-0119
Fax Number: (0117) 956-7424
Ground Capacity: 2,500
Seating Capacity: 300
Web: www.pitchero.com/clubs/mangotsfieldunited

GENERAL INFORMATION
Car Parking: 80 spaces available at the ground
Coach Parking: At the nearby Cleeve Rugby Ground
Nearest Railway Station: Bristol Parkway (5 miles)
Nearest Bus Station: Central Bristol (7 miles)
Club Shop: At the ground
Opening Times: Matchdays only
Telephone Nº: (0117) 956-0119

GROUND INFORMATION
Away Supporters' Entrances & Sections:
No usual segregation

ADMISSION INFO (2011/2012 PRICES)
Adult Standing/Seating: £8.00
Senior Citizen Standing/Seating: £5.00
Under-16s Standing/Seating: £3.00
Programme Price: £1.50

DISABLED INFORMATION
Wheelchairs: Accommodated at the front of the stand
Helpers: Admitted
Prices: Standard prices apply
Disabled Toilets: Available in the Clubhouse
Contact: (0117) 956-0119 (Bookings are necessary)

Travelling Supporters' Information:
Routes: Exit the M32 at Junction 1 and follow the A4174 Ring Road through the traffic lights at the crossroads. At the first roundabout turn left and continue on the A4174. Carry straight on at the second roundabout then turn right at the third roundabout onto the Westerleigh Road, passing the Beefeater pub on the right and the Shell Garage on the left. Cross the mini-roundabout then turn left at the traffic lights into Blackhorse Road. Continue across another mini-roundabout into Richmond Road then turn left at the T-junction with St. James Street opposite the Red Lion. Continue for approximately 150 yards then take the 2nd turning on the left into Cossham Street. The ground is approximately 400 yards down the road on the right.

NORTH LEIGH FC

Founded: 1908
Former Names: None
Nickname: 'The Millers'
Ground: Eynsham Hall Sports Park, North Leigh, Witney OX29 6SL
Record Attendance: 426 (16th October 2004)

Colours: Yellow shirts with Black shorts
Telephone No: 07583 399577
Ground Capacity: 2,000
Seating Capacity: 175
Web Site: www.pitchero.com/clubs/northleighfc

GENERAL INFORMATION
Car Parking: At the ground
Coach Parking: At the ground
Nearest Railway Station: Hanborough (2½ miles)
Club Shop: None
Opening Times: –
Telephone No: –

GROUND INFORMATION
Away Supporters' Entrances & Sections:
No usual segregation

ADMISSION INFO (2011/2012 PRICES)
Adult Standing: £7.00
Adult Seating: £7.00
Senior Citizen/Junior Standing: £3.50
Senior Citizen/Junior Seating: £3.50
Under-16s Standing/Seating: Free of charge when accompanied by a paying adult
Programme Price: £1.00

DISABLED INFORMATION
Wheelchairs: Accommodated
Helpers: Admitted
Prices: Normal prices apply for the disabled. Helpers are admitted free of charge
Disabled Toilets: Available
Contact: 07583 399577 (Bookings are not necessary)

Travelling Supporters' Information:
Routes: Exit the M40 at Junction 9 and take the A34 towards Oxford. After about 5 miles take the slip road to the Peartree Interchange and head northwards on the A44 signposted for Woodstock & Evesham. Continue along the A44 and, shortly after passing Oxford Airport on the right, then turn left onto the A4095 at the roundabout. Continue down the A4095 passing through Long Hanborough and the entrance to the ground is located on the left as you enter North Leigh village.

PAULTON ROVERS FC

Founded: 1881
Former Names: None
Nickname: 'The Rovers'
Ground: Athletic Ground, Winterfield Road, Paulton, Bristol BS39 7RF
Record Attendance: 2,070 (vs Norwich City, 2009)
Colours: Shirts and shorts are White with Maroon trim
Telephone Nº: (01761) 412907
Ground Capacity: 5,000
Seating Capacity: 253
Web Site: www.paultonrovers.co.uk

GENERAL INFORMATION
Car Parking: At the ground
Coach Parking: At the ground
Nearest Railway Station: Oldfield Park (9½ miles)
Club Shop: None
Opening Times: –
Telephone Nº: –

GROUND INFORMATION
Away Supporters' Entrances & Sections: No usual segregation

ADMISSION INFO (2011/2012 PRICES)
Adult Standing: £8.00
Adult Seating: £8.00
Senior Citizen/Junior Standing: £5.00
Senior Citizen/Junior Seating: £5.00
Note: Under-16s are admitted free of charge when accompanying a paying adult
Programme Price: £2.00

DISABLED INFORMATION
Wheelchairs: Accommodated
Helpers: Admitted
Prices: Normal prices apply for the disabled. Helpers are admitted free of charge
Disabled Toilets: Available in the Clubhouse
Contact: (01761) 412907 (Bookings are not necessary)

Travelling Supporters' Information:
Routes: Paulton is located to the south of Bristol just to the east of the A37. Take the A37 to Farrington Gurney and turn off onto the A363. Continue to the crossroads with the B3355 and turn left, heading northwards into Paulton. Pass the hospital, continue into Winterfield Road and entrance to the ground is on the right, shortly after bend in the road.

POOLE TOWN FC

Founded: 1880
Former Names: Various names including Poole FC and Poole St. Marys FC
Nickname: 'The Dolphins'
Ground: Tatnam Farm, School Lane, Poole, BH15 3JR
Record Attendance: 1,652 (26/3/2011 at Tatnam)
Pitch Size: 110 × 73 yards

Colours: Red & White halved shirts with Red shorts
Telephone N°: (01794) 517991
Matchday Contact N°: 07771 604289
Office Address: 153 High Street, Poole BH15 1AU
Ground Capacity: 2,000
Seating Capacity: 152
Web Site: www.pooletownfc.co.uk

GENERAL INFORMATION
Car Parking: At the ground
Coach Parking: At the ground
Nearest Railway Station: Poole (¾ mile)
Nearest Bus Station: Poole
Club Shop: At the ground
Opening Times: Matchdays only
Telephone N°: 07771 604289

GROUND INFORMATION
Away Supporters' Entrances & Sections:
No usual segregation

ADMISSION INFO (2011/2012 PRICES)
Adult Standing: £8.00
Adult Seating: £8.00
Senior Citizen/Junior Standing: £5.00
Senior Citizen/Junior Seating: £5.00
Junior Standing: £2.00
Junior Seating: £2.00
Programme Price: £2.00

DISABLED INFORMATION
Wheelchairs: Accommodated
Helpers: Admitted
Prices: Normal prices apply for the disabled and helpers
Disabled Toilets: One available
Contact: (01794) 517991   (Bookings are not necessary)

Travelling Supporters' Information:
Routes: Take the A35, A3049 or the A349 into Poole to the Fleetsbridge Interchange where these roads all meet. At the interchange, takes the Fleets Lane exit and head southwards into the centre of Poole. Continue along Fleets Lane into Stanley Green Road (passing the Retail Park and part of the Industrial Estate) for approximately ½ mile then turn left into Palmer Road. Take the first turning on the right into School Lane for the ground.

SHOLING FC

Founded: 1884
Former Names: Vosper Thornycroft FC, VT FC and a number of other earlier names
Nickname: 'The Boatmen'
Ground: VT Group Sports Ground, Portsmouth Road, Old Netley, Southampton SO19 9PW
Record Attendance: 585 (vs Salisbury City, 2006/07)

Colours: Red and White striped shirts with Red shorts
Telephone Nº: (023) 8040-3829
Ground Capacity: 2,000
Seating Capacity: 150
Web Site: www.pitchero.com/clubs/vtfc

GENERAL INFORMATION
Car Parking: At the ground
Coach Parking: At the ground
Nearest Railway Station: Sholing (1½ miles)
Club Shop: None
Opening Times: –
Telephone Nº: –

GROUND INFORMATION
Away Supporters' Entrances & Sections:
No usual segregation

ADMISSION INFO (2011/2012 PRICES)
Adult Standing: £8.00
Adult Seating: £8.00
Senior Citizen/Child Standing: £2.00
Senior Citizen/Child Seating: £2.00
Note: Children are admitted free of charge when accompanied by a paying adult
Programme Price: £2.00

DISABLED INFORMATION
Wheelchairs: Accommodated
Helpers: Admitted
Prices: Normal prices apply for the disabled and helpers
Disabled Toilets: Available
Contact: (023) 8040-3829 (Bookings are not necessary)

Travelling Supporters' Information:
Routes: Exit the M27 at Junction 8 and take the 2nd exit at the roundabout into A3025 Hamble Lane. After around ½ mile, turn right into Portsmouth Road (still the A3025) and the ground is on the right hand side of the road after ½ mile.

STOURPORT SWIFTS FC

Founded: 1882
Former Names: None
Nickname: 'The Swifts'
Ground: Walshes Meadow, Harold Davies Drive, Stourport-on-Severn DY13 0AA
Record Attendance: 2,000

Colours: Black and Gold striped shirts with Black shorts
Telephone Nº: (01299) 825188
Ground Capacity: 2,000
Seating Capacity: 250
Web Site: www.stourportswiftsfc.co.uk

GENERAL INFORMATION
Car Parking: At the ground
Coach Parking: At the ground
Nearest Railway Station: Hartlebury (3½ miles) or Kidderminster (4½ miles)
Club Shop: None
Opening Times: –
Telephone Nº: –

GROUND INFORMATION
Away Supporters' Entrances & Sections:
No usual segregation

ADMISSION INFO (2011/2012 PRICES)
Adult Standing: £6.00
Adult Seating: £6.00
Senior Citizen/Junior Standing: £3.00
Senior Citizen/Junior Seating: £3.00
Note: Under-12s are admitted free of charge when accompanied by a paying adult
Programme Price: £1.50

DISABLED INFORMATION
Wheelchairs: Accommodated
Helpers: Admitted
Prices: Normal prices apply for the disabled and helpers
Disabled Toilets: None
Contact: (01299) 825188 (Bookings are not necessary)

Travelling Supporters' Information:
Routes: Take the A451 from Kidderminster to Stourport and follow this road along the one-way system through the town centre (follow signposts for the Sports Centre). Cross over the River Severn Bridge, turn left into Harold Davies Drive and the Sports Centre is on the left. The football ground is located at the rear of the Sports Centre.

TAUNTON TOWN FC

Founded: 1947
Former Names: None
Nickname: 'The Peacocks'
Ground: Wordsworth Drive, Taunton TA1 2HG
Record Attendance: 3,284 (1999)

Colours: Sky Blue shirts with Claret shorts
Telephone Nº: (01823) 278191
Fax Number: (01823) 278191
Ground Capacity: 2,500
Seating Capacity: 300
Web Site: www.tauntontown.com

GENERAL INFORMATION
Car Parking: At the ground
Coach Parking: At the ground
Nearest Railway Station: Taunton (1¼ miles)
Club Shop: None
Opening Times: –
Telephone Nº: –

GROUND INFORMATION
Away Supporters' Entrances & Sections:
No usual segregation

ADMISSION INFO (2011/2012 PRICES)
Adult Standing: £7.00
Adult Seating: £7.00
Senior Citizen/Student Standing: £5.00
Senior Citizen/Student Seating: £5.00
Under-16s Standing/Seating: £2.00
Programme Price: £1.50

DISABLED INFORMATION
Wheelchairs: Accommodated
Helpers: Admitted
Prices: Normal prices apply for the disabled. Helpers pay concessionary prices
Disabled Toilets: Available
Contact: (01823) 278191   (Bookings are not necessary)

Travelling Supporters' Information:
Routes: Exit the M5 at Junction 25 and follow signs for Taunton Town Centre. Bear left at the first set of traffic lights then go straight on at the next set of traffic lights into Wordsworth Drive. The ground is on the left hand side of the road after approximately 200 yards.

THATCHAM TOWN FC

Unfortunately, no ground photograph for Thatcham Town FC was available at the time of going to press.

Founded: 1895
Former Names: None
Nickname: 'The Kingfishers'
Ground: Waterside Park, Crookham Hill, Thatcham, RG19 4PA
Record Attendance: 1,400

Colours: Blue and White striped shirts with Blue shorts
Telephone N°: (01635) 862016
Fax Number: (01635) 873934
Ground Capacity: 3,000
Seating Capacity: 300
Web Site: www.thatchamtownfc.co.uk

GENERAL INFORMATION
Car Parking: At the ground
Coach Parking: At the ground
Nearest Railway Station: Thatcham (¼ mile)
Club Shop: At the ground
Opening Times: Matchdays only
Telephone N°: –

GROUND INFORMATION
Away Supporters' Entrances & Sections:
No usual segregation

ADMISSION INFO (2011/2012 PRICES)
Adult Standing: £7.00
Adult Seating: £7.00
Senior Citizen Standing: £4.00
Senior Citizen Seating: £4.00
Under-16s Standing/Seating: £1.00
Programme Price: £1.50

DISABLED INFORMATION
Wheelchairs: Accommodated
Helpers: Admitted
Prices: Normal prices apply for the disabled and helpers
Disabled Toilets: Available
Contact: (01635) 862016   (Bookings are not necessary)

Travelling Supporters' Information:
Routes: Thatcham is situated on the A4 between Newbury and Reading. Take the A4 to Thatcham then head south along Pipers Way at the roundabout to the eastern side of Thatcham. At the bottom of Pipers Way, turn left at the roundabout into Station Road, cross the railway line and bear right where the road forks before turning off immediately on the left for the entrance to the ground.

TIVERTON TOWN FC

Founded: 1920
Former Names: None
Nickname: 'Tivvy'
Ground: Ladysmead, Bolham Road, Tiverton, EX16 6SG
Record Attendance: 3,000 (1994)

Colours: Yellow shirts and shorts
Telephone Nº: (01884) 252397
Ground Capacity: 3,000
Seating Capacity: 520
Web site: www.tivertontownfc.com

GENERAL INFORMATION
Car Parking: At the ground
Coach Parking: At the ground
Nearest Railway Station: Tiverton Parkway (7 miles)
Nearest Bus Station: Tiverton
Club Shop: At the ground
Opening Times: Matchdays only
Telephone Nº: (01884) 252397

GROUND INFORMATION
Away Supporters' Entrances & Sections:
No usual segregation

ADMISSION INFO (2011/2012 PRICES)
Adult Standing: £8.00
Adult Seating: £9.00
Under-16s Standing: £1.00
Under-16s Seating: £2.00
Senior Citizen Standing: £5.50
Senior Citizen Seating: £6.50
Programme Price: £2.00

DISABLED INFORMATION
Wheelchairs: Accommodated
Helpers: Admitted
Prices: Normal prices apply
Disabled Toilets: Available
Contact: (01884) 252397 (Bookings are not necessary)

Travelling Supporters' Information:
Routes: Exit the M5 at Junction 27 and follow the A361 towards Tiverton for about 7 miles. Ignore the first junction for the A396 (Tiverton and Bickleigh) at Gornhay Cross and keep going until you reach a large roundabout. Turn left at the roundabout (A3126) for the Town Centre and Castle and continue along for about 400 yards. Cross the new roundabout passing the College Sports Field and Rugby Club and the ground is then on the right just by R & M Cars.

WIMBORNE TOWN FC

Photo courtesy of seekerphoto.co.uk

Founded: 1878
Former Names: None
Nickname: 'The Magpies'
Ground: Cuthbury, Cowgrove Road, Wimborne Minster   BH21 4EL
Record Attendance: 3,250

Colours: Black & White striped shirts with Black shorts
Telephone Nº: (01202) 884821
Fax Number: (01202) 888023
Ground Capacity: 3,250
Seating Capacity: 275
Web Site: www.wimbornetownfc.co.uk

GENERAL INFORMATION
Car Parking: At the ground
Coach Parking: At the ground
Nearest Railway Station: Hamworth (9½ miles)
Club Shop: At the ground
Opening Times: Matchdays only
Telephone Nº: (01202) 884821

GROUND INFORMATION
Away Supporters' Entrances & Sections:
No usual segregation

ADMISSION INFO (2011/2012 PRICES)
Adult Standing: £8.00
Adult Seating: £8.00
Senior Citizen Standing: £4.50
Senior Citizen Seating: £4.50
Under-16s Standing/Seating: £1.00
Programme Price: £1.20

DISABLED INFORMATION
Wheelchairs: Accommodated
Helpers: Admitted
Prices: Normal prices apply for the disabled and helpers
Disabled Toilets: To become available during 2010/11
Contact: (01202) 884821   (Bookings are not necessary)

Travelling Supporters' Information:
Routes: The ground is located on the western outskirts of Wimborne Minster which is situated just to the north of the A31. Take the A31 to the junction with with A349 then head north on the B3073 passing over the River Stour into Poole Road. Continue along the B3073 into Rodway, turn left at the roundabout into Lewens Lane and left again into Park Lane. Follow the road around right into East Street (still the B3073) and continue into King Street before taking the second exit at the roundabout into Victoria Road (B3082). Continue along this road then turn left into Cowgrove Road. The entrance to the ground is on the left after a short distance.

YATE TOWN FC

Founded: 1906 **(Re-formed:** 1946)
Former Names: Yate Rovers FC, Yate YMCA FC
Nickname: 'Bluebells'
Ground: Lodge Road, Yate BS37 7LE
Record Attendance: 2,000
Pitch Size: 117 × 76 yards

Colours: White shirts with Navy Blue shorts
Telephone Nº: (01454) 228103
Fax Number: (01454) 324305
Ground Capacity: 2,000
Seating Capacity: 250
Web site: www.yatetownfc.com

GENERAL INFORMATION
Car Parking: Large car park available at the ground
Coach Parking: At the ground
Nearest Railway Station: Yate
Nearest Bus Station: Bristol
Club Shop: At the ground
Opening Times: Matchdays only
Telephone Nº: (01454) 324305 (Club secretary)

GROUND INFORMATION
Away Supporters' Entrances & Sections:
No usual segregation

ADMISSION INFO (2011/2012 PRICES)
Adult Standing: £7.00
Adult Seating: £7.00
Senior Citizen/Under-16s Standing: £4.00
Senior Citizen/Under-16s Seating: £4.00
Under-11s Standing/Seating: £1.00 when accompanied by a paying adult
Programme Price: £1.50

DISABLED INFORMATION
Wheelchairs: Accommodated
Helpers: One helper admitted per disabled fan
Prices: Free of charge for the disabled and helpers
Disabled Toilets: Available in the Clubhouse
Contact: (01454) 228103 (Bookings are not necessary)

Travelling Supporters' Information:
Routes: From the East: Exit the M4 at Junction 18 and enter Yate on the A432 via the Chipping Sodbury bypass. Turn right at the first roundabout (into Link Road), carry straight on over the next roundabout into Goose Green Way and over two more roundabouts and through two sets of traffic lights. At the third set of lights turn right then immediately left into Lodge Road. The ground is on the right after 200 yards; From the North/Midlands: Exit the M5 at Junction 14 and take the B4509/B4060 into Chipping Sodbury. Turn right into the High Street and continue down Bowling Hill then turn right at the first roundabout into Goose Green Way. Then as above.

Southern Football League Premier Division 2010/2011 Season

	Banbury United	Bashley	Bedford Town	Brackley Town	Cambridge City	Chesham United	Chippenham Town	Cirencester Town	Didcot Town	Evesham United	Halesowen Town	Hednesford Town	Hemel Hempstead Town	Leamington	Oxford City	Salisbury City	Stourbridge	Swindon Supermarine	Tiverton Town	Truro City	Weymouth
Banbury United		1-4	2-0	0-0	2-0	2-1	1-2	0-2	2-1	1-1	0-2	0-4	0-4	1-1	0-2	0-1	4-0	0-0	2-2	0-3	3-0
Bashley	2-1		2-5	0-3	1-1	1-1	1-4	1-2	1-1	1-0	0-0	0-4	1-0	0-4	3-1	0-2	0-0	2-0	1-0	2-1	5-1
Bedford Town	0-1	1-0		2-1	1-2	1-2	1-1	1-6	1-1	1-2	0-0	2-1	0-1	0-2	0-1	1-0	2-1	0-6	1-3	1-1	4-1
Brackley Town	2-0	3-4	4-0		0-0	1-1	1-1	4-1	2-1	5-0	6-0	0-0	3-1	0-0	1-0	0-3	0-0	1-4	1-0	3-2	1-1
Cambridge City	1-1	1-1	2-0	2-3		0-0	0-1	1-2	4-2	2-0	7-1	3-2	3-2	3-2	3-0	3-3	3-0	2-0	5-0	0-1	1-0
Chesham United	0-2	0-0	0-0	1-0	1-0		2-0	6-1	1-1	1-0	3-0	2-1	3-3	1-0	2-0	1-1	2-0	4-0	5-0	1-0	2-1
Chippenham Town	4-0	1-0	3-1	3-2	1-0	1-0		0-0	1-1	1-0	3-1	0-1	2-0	0-0	1-2	1-1	0-0	3-1	4-1	1-2	1-0
Cirencester Town	1-1	2-1	4-2	0-3	1-2	3-2	1-1		0-0	1-2	5-0	0-1	3-2	0-1	4-1	0-3	1-2	1-2	1-0	0-3	3-0
Didcot Town	0-2	0-2	1-0	1-1	1-2	1-0	1-1	1-2		1-2	1-1	0-3	0-1	1-2	0-3	1-1	1-4	1-4	2-0	0-3	2-2
Evesham United	4-3	2-2	0-0	1-0	1-2	0-0	2-2	2-1	3-0		0-0	4-1	1-0	0-1	3-0	0-0	2-3	0-1	3-1	3-4	1-3
Halesowen Town	3-1	0-2	0-3	5-3	0-1	1-4	1-2	1-1	1-0	0-8		0-6	1-6	0-3	0-3	0-4	0-3	1-1	0-1	0-3	0-0
Hednesford Town	1-0	1-0	4-1	2-0	0-2	3-2	0-2	3-1	1-1	1-0	4-2		2-0	1-1	2-1	3-0	2-3	1-1	2-0	1-0	9-0
Hemel Hempstead Town	1-2	0-2	1-0	1-0	0-2	0-1	1-2	2-2	0-1	1-0	1-0	0-1		1-0	0-2	0-3	2-2	1-2	2-1	1-1	1-2
Leamington	3-1	2-1	5-0	2-1	2-3	3-2	0-0	1-0	2-1	1-0	3-0	1-2	2-3		2-0	2-0	3-2	2-0	2-1	3-2	1-0
Oxford City	2-2	1-1	1-1	0-2	0-1	0-2	0-0	3-3	0-3	0-1	0-0	1-1	3-0	2-3		2-2	0-2	2-1	3-1	1-1	5-0
Salisbury City	4-1	2-1	4-1	3-1	1-3	3-2	4-0	4-1	4-2	0-3	7-1	2-1	1-1	0-0	2-0		3-0	2-0	3-0	0-6	3-2
Stourbridge	2-1	6-1	3-0	2-1	3-0	1-1	1-0	2-1	3-1	3-1	0-2	1-2	1-5	4-3	0-3	0-0		5-1	0-0	2-2	7-2
Swindon Supermarine	3-0	4-2	1-0	1-5	0-2	0-0	3-1	1-0	2-0	1-1	3-0	1-2	1-3	1-0	1-1	1-2	2-1		3-0	0-2	0-1
Tiverton Town	1-0	2-2	3-5	1-3	2-2	1-2	0-0	2-2	2-3	1-0	0-0	1-2	1-0	1-0	0-0	1-3	1-0	0-1		1-2	0-4
Truro City	1-0	2-1	0-1	1-0	2-0	0-3	5-0	2-0	2-1	1-1	6-0	1-0	3-0	3-1	2-1	1-1	3-1	7-2	3-0		3-2
Weymouth	2-4	1-4	3-1	0-0	0-3	3-0	3-3	1-0	1-2	2-0	3-0	2-4	2-2	1-2	1-1	2-0	3-2	0-0	3-1	0-4	

Southern Football League Division One Central 2010/2011 Season

	AFC Hayes	Arlesey Town	Ashford Town (Middlesex)	Atherstone Town	Aylesbury	Barton Rovers	Beaconsfield SYCOB	Bedfont Town	Bedworth United	Biggleswade Town	Burnham	Daventry Town	Hitchin Town	Leighton Town	Marlow	North Greenford United	Northwood	Rugby Town	Slough Town	Soham Town Rangers	Uxbridge	Woodford United
AFC Hayes	■	1-2	0-2	6-2	0-1	1-1	1-1	1-2	2-0	2-1	2-0	2-2	0-5	0-4	2-2	2-3	4-2	0-4	2-4	2-0	2-1	1-2
Arlesey Town	3-0	■	2-0	12-0	4-0	2-1	1-0	3-0	3-0	0-0	8-0	0-1	1-2	1-1	3-1	5-0	2-1	4-1	2-1	6-1	3-1	3-2
Ashford Town (Middlesex)	4-2	0-3	■	1-1	1-2	1-0	3-1	1-1	2-2	2-3	2-2	1-4	3-0	0-3	0-3	3-2	0-0	3-4	1-2	4-2	3-0	2-3
Atherstone Town	2-1	0-3	1-3	■	3-1	3-1	1-3	0-3	0-1	0-3	2-3	1-2	1-3	1-2	0-7	2-0	4-0	1-1	1-2	3-4	3-3	0-4
Aylesbury	4-1	2-2	1-3	4-2	■	2-0	2-2	0-1	0-1	2-2	3-0	1-0	1-3	1-1	1-0	0-0	3-2	1-3	1-2	1-5	4-3	1-1
Barton Rovers	1-2	1-2	6-2	0-1	0-1	■	2-2	4-1	3-1	4-2	0-0	2-3	2-5	0-1	1-0	1-3	1-1	1-1	2-0	1-0	2-1	0-1
Beaconsfield SYCOB	4-3	2-3	2-3	1-2	1-1	0-1	■	1-1	3-1	0-1	0-2	3-5	1-4	1-0	1-1	2-3	0-1	1-2	1-0	1-3	0-0	4-2
Bedfont Town	3-1	0-0	2-5	1-1	1-1	1-0	4-2	■	3-2	2-1	2-1	0-0	1-1	1-0	1-1	7-0	3-1	2-3	1-2	2-1	1-1	0-3
Bedworth United	1-1	1-2	2-1	1-2	1-3	0-1	0-0	2-0	■	1-2	0-1	0-0	2-1	2-1	1-0	1-1	1-1	1-0	2-1			
Biggleswade Town	4-0	2-2	4-0	5-1	2-4	3-1	2-1	1-0	3-4	■	5-2	1-0	1-2	2-1	3-1	2-0	6-2	1-1	1-5	1-1	2-1	1-0
Burnham	0-2	1-2	1-0	6-1	0-3	3-3	0-2	1-1	2-1	2-1	■	2-2	1-2	3-1	1-3	5-3	2-3	2-1	0-2	0-4	1-1	2-1
Daventry Town	3-1	1-1	4-2	3-1	1-0	5-0	1-0	5-1	2-2	1-2	2-0	■	1-1	2-0	0-1	3-2	4-1	4-2	1-2	0-0	4-1	3-2
Hitchin Town	2-0	0-1	3-3	5-2	4-2	1-2	4-0	5-1	1-2	3-0	2-0	5-0	■	3-0	2-0	1-0	1-2	3-2	9-1	2-2		0-0
Leighton Town	2-1	1-2	3-0	2-2	0-0	4-1	0-0	3-1	1-0	0-3	1-1	5-0	3-2	■	1-1	1-1	5-0	4-1	3-1	4-1	2-1	2-1
Marlow	4-1	1-1	2-1	2-0	1-3	0-5	0-0	1-2	4-1	0-0	2-3	1-2	1-1	1-1	■	3-0	1-2	0-3	1-4	1-0	4-7	0-1
North Greenford United	1-2	2-0	2-0	3-3	1-1	2-2	2-0	1-1	2-2	1-1	1-0	0-3	1-5	1-0	1-3	■	0-2	0-2	1-3	2-1	2-2	2-3
Northwood	3-1	1-5	2-2	2-5	1-1	1-2	2-1	5-2	3-4	0-3	3-1	0-6	0-7	1-3	1-6	0-1	■	0-0	1-5	2-1	0-2	5-0
Rugby Town	4-0	1-3	0-1	3-1	0-2	2-2	1-1	4-2	1-0	0-0	1-4	1-4	1-1	2-2	2-0	2-1	1-0	■	1-0	5-1	4-0	0-0
Slough Town	5-0	0-3	2-0	3-0	3-2	2-1	6-4	1-1	2-1	3-2	2-3	1-3	1-1	0-1	1-3	2-1	4-3	1-3	■	2-1	5-2	3-3
Soham Town Rangers	0-0	0-1	1-1	3-1	1-2	0-1	0-0	1-0	2-2	0-3	0-2	2-3	3-3	1-2	2-0	3-1	1-4	1-0		■	2-2	3-0
Uxbridge	0-2	2-1	3-2	1-2	1-3	1-0	3-0	1-3	2-3	1-4	4-2	1-6	1-0	3-1	1-2	3-1	2-2	3-0	2-1	5-1	■	5-1
Woodford United	5-0	2-1	2-1	4-2	2-5	0-0	1-0	0-3	0-0	1-3	3-0	0-0	0-0	2-0	1-0	2-1	0-1	0-0	1-3	1-0	3-0	■

Southern Football League Division One South & West 2010/2011 Season

	Abingdon United	AFC Totton	Almondsbury Town	Andover	Bideford	Bishops Cleeve	Bridgwater Town	Cinderford Town	Clevedon Town	Frome Town	Gosport Borough	Hungerford Town	Mangotsfield United	North Leigh	Paulton Rovers	Sholing	Stourport Swifts	Taunton Town	Thatcham Town	Wimborne Town	Yate Town
Abingdon United		1-0	1-2	1-2	0-2	2-1	1-2	5-4	2-0	1-4	1-3	2-2	1-3	2-0	1-1	0-1	1-1	1-3	0-3	0-0	3-1
AFC Totton	7-0		3-0	9-0	5-1	0-0	4-2	3-1	0-1	3-2	5-2	7-0	1-2	3-1	5-1	2-1	3-2	3-1	3-0	5-2	4-1
Almondsbury Town	3-1	1-0		3-2	1-5	0-0	4-0	2-0	1-0	0-1	4-0	0-0	3-3	1-0	2-0	0-0	2-2	0-2	3-2	3-2	3-1
Andover	1-5	0-2	0-2		3-4	0-5	0-4	1-2	1-2	0-3	0-1	0-3	0-2	1-4	0-3	0-0	1-2	2-2	0-2	1-3	0-1
Bideford	4-2	1-1	0-0	2-1		2-0	0-2	0-3	3-1	1-4	2-0	0-0	3-4	0-2	3-0	2-5	1-1	1-2	1-1	1-2	2-1
Bishops Cleeve	2-2	0-2	2-2	2-0	1-2		1-1	0-1	1-1	0-1	3-0	1-0	1-2	3-3	1-5	0-0	0-0	0-0	3-0	0-1	2-1
Bridgwater Town	0-3	0-3	2-2	1-0	3-1	1-1		2-3	1-4	2-5	4-2	1-2	0-2	4-0	0-2	0-4	0-0	0-0	0-4	0-1	0-5
Cinderford Town	3-2	1-2	1-0	2-2	0-3	4-0	1-0		4-1	1-0	1-1	2-2	1-3	1-2	3-3	2-0	3-2	1-2	0-4	5-1	0-0
Clevedon Town	2-2	2-2	2-3	5-0	2-2	1-4	1-1	0-2		1-3	1-1	1-3	1-2	2-3	0-2	2-3	1-3	0-3	2-1	1-0	0-1
Frome Town	5-0	0-3	1-4	3-0	0-2	1-1	6-0	4-0	2-1		2-1	0-1	2-0	8-0	1-0	1-0	1-1	0-0	2-0	3-1	0-0
Gosport Borough	3-2	0-1	1-1	1-2	4-1	1-0	1-1	1-0	3-1	1-0		1-1	1-3	2-1	3-3	1-1	3-0	2-0	2-1	3-2	2-1
Hungerford Town	3-2	0-3	4-1	6-1	3-0	1-2	2-0	0-0	2-0	0-1	3-0		0-1	1-2	0-0	0-1	4-1	1-0	0-0	1-1	1-0
Mangotsfield United	4-0	1-2	1-1	1-1	4-0	3-1	2-2	3-2	2-1	0-2	3-2	2-0		3-3	1-1	1-2	1-0	1-0	4-2	3-2	0-1
North Leigh	1-1	0-3	5-4	2-1	5-4	6-2	6-3	1-1	5-2	1-2	1-2	1-1	1-2		1-1	0-4	4-2	0-2	0-3	2-1	2-2
Paulton Rovers	0-2	1-3	4-1	2-1	0-0	2-1	3-0	1-0	2-2	1-1	2-0	1-4	0-1	3-4		1-6	3-0	1-0	2-2	2-1	2-1
Sholing	4-1	2-0	2-1	3-0	2-0	6-1	6-0	1-0	2-1	2-1	3-2	1-0	1-0	1-2	2-1		4-1	5-0	2-1	3-0	2-0
Stourport Swifts	0-1	0-5	1-1	4-2	1-4	2-0	1-1	2-1	1-0	1-2	0-2	4-4	0-2	0-4	3-3	1-3		1-3	0-1	3-1	0-3
Taunton Town	3-1	1-4	1-0	2-1	2-3	2-0	1-1	1-3	1-1	1-0	3-1	1-1	3-1	0-0	3-2	1-1	1-3		0-2	0-0	0-2
Thatcham Town	4-0	1-4	1-0	2-0	3-0	1-0	1-1	1-1	5-0	0-0	1-0	2-0	3-4	1-2	3-0	1-0	3-4	1-0		0-1	1-1
Wimborne Town	0-3	1-4	0-1	4-3	1-3	0-4	1-2	2-1	5-0	0-3	3-2	0-1	1-1	1-2	1-1	1-3	1-0	0-2	1-4		0-3
Yate Town	1-0	2-2	1-1	2-2	1-2	0-1	0-3	1-2	2-0	0-0	1-0	0-1	0-1	1-2	0-2	0-1	1-2	2-0	0-2	2-0	

76

Southern Football League
Premier Division
Season 2010/2011

Team	P	W	D	L	F	A	Pts
Truro City	40	27	6	7	91	35	87
Hednesford Town	40	26	5	9	82	38	83
Salisbury City	40	23	10	7	82	45	79
Cambridge City	40	24	7	9	74	40	79
Leamington	40	24	6	10	68	39	78
Chesham United	40	20	11	9	64	35	71
Chippenham Town	40	18	14	8	54	41	68
Stourbridge	40	18	8	14	72	61	62
Brackley Town	40	16	10	14	67	47	58
Swindon Supermarine	40	17	7	16	56	58	58
Bashley	40	14	10	16	55	63	52
Evesham United	40	14	9	17	54	49	51
Cirencester Town	40	13	8	19	59	67	47
Oxford City	40	11	12	17	48	54	45
Hemel Hempstead Town	40	13	6	21	50	59	45
Banbury United	40	11	8	21	44	67	40
Bedford Town	40	10	7	23	41	76	37
Weymouth	40	12	8	20	55	85	34
Didcot Town	40	7	11	22	39	69	32
Tiverton Town	40	7	8	25	33	77	29
Halesowen Town	40	5	9	26	24	107	24

Weymouth had 10 points deducted.
Banbury United had 1 point deducted.
Windsor & Eton was wound up in the High Court on 2nd February 2011, due to unpaid taxes. The club's record was expunged on 8th February 2011:   26   8   12   6   33   35   36

Promotion Play-offs

Hednesford Town 3   Leamington 1
Salisbury City 1   Cambridge City 0

Hednesford Town 2   Salisbury City .... 2 (aet.)
Salisbury City won 3-2 on penalties

Promoted: Truro City and Salisbury City

Relegated: Didcot Town, Tiverton Town and Halesowen Town

Southern Football League
Division One Central
Season 2010/2011

Arlesey Town	42	30	7	5	108	34	88
Hitchin Town	42	26	9	7	107	44	87
Daventry Town	42	26	9	7	95	47	81
Biggleswade Town	42	24	9	9	89	51	81
Slough Town	42	24	4	14	91	66	76
Rugby Town	42	20	11	11	74	56	71
Leighton Town	42	19	12	11	72	50	69
Aylesbury	42	19	11	12	73	62	68
Woodford United	42	18	9	15	61	59	63
Bedfont Town	42	17	12	13	66	66	63
Marlow	42	15	9	18	68	65	54
Barton Rovers	42	14	9	19	59	64	51
Uxbridge	42	14	8	20	76	87	50
Burnham	42	14	7	21	61	87	49
Bedworth United	42	12	12	18	49	62	48
Ashford Town	42	13	8	21	69	85	47
Soham Town Rangers	42	10	10	22	55	81	40
North Greenford United	42	10	10	22	51	86	40
AFC Hayes	42	11	6	25	54	96	39
Northwood	42	11	6	25	59	106	39
Atherstone Town	42	10	6	26	61	118	36
Beaconsfield SYCOB	42	7	12	23	49	75	33

Arlesey Town had 9 points deducted.
Daventry Town had 6 points deducted.
Atherstone Town resigned from the League at the end of the season.
Soham Town Rangers transferred to the Isthmian League Division One North at the end of the season.

Promotion Play-offs

Hitchin Town .... 4 Slough Town 2
Daventry Town .... 2 Biggleswade Town 0

Hitchin Town .... 2 Daventry Town 0

Promoted: Arlesey Town and Hitchin Town

Southern Football League
Division One South & West
Season 2010/2011

AFC Totton	40	31	4	5	121	35	97
Sholing	40	30	5	5	90	27	95
Mangotsfield United	40	26	7	7	79	48	85
Frome Town	40	24	7	9	77	31	79
Thatcham Town	40	20	7	13	70	43	67
North Leigh	40	19	8	13	81	81	65
Hungerford Town	40	17	12	11	58	43	63
Almondsbury Town	40	17	12	11	62	54	63
Taunton Town	40	16	10	14	49	49	58
Bideford	40	17	7	16	68	73	58
Paulton Rovers	40	15	12	13	64	63	57
Cinderford Town	40	16	8	16	63	61	56
Gosport Borough	40	16	7	17	58	65	55
Yate Town	40	12	8	20	43	48	44
Bishop's Cleeve	40	10	12	18	47	59	42
Abingdon United	40	11	7	22	56	85	40
Stourport Swifts	40	10	10	20	52	81	40
Bridgwater Town	40	9	11	20	47	86	38
Wimborne Town	40	10	5	25	45	81	35
Clevedon Town	40	6	8	26	46	86	26
Andover	40	2	5	33	32	109	11

Almondsbury Town resigned from the League at the end of the season.
Andover resigned from the League shortly before the start of the 2011/2012 season.

Promotion Play-offs

Sholing .... 2 Thatcham Town 0
Mangotsfield United .... 1 Frome Town 3

Sholing .... 0 Frome Town 1

Promoted: AFC Totton and Frome Town

F.A. Trophy 2010/2011

Qualifying 1	AFC Hornchurch	2	Brentwood Town	1
Qualifying 1	AFC Totton	5	AFC Hayes	0
Qualifying 1	Almondsbury Town	1	Didcot Town	0
Qualifying 1	Arlesey Town	0	Ramsgate	0
Qualifying 1	Ashford Town (Middlesex)	6	North Greenford United	2
Qualifying 1	Banbury United	1	Wimborne Town	1
Qualifying 1	Bideford	4	Tiverton Town	2
Qualifying 1	Biggleswade Town	0	Billericay Town	1
Qualifying 1	Bognor Regis Town	1	Croydon Athletic	0
Qualifying 1	Bridgwater Town	1	Stourbridge	3
Qualifying 1	Burnham	0	Brackley Town	0
Qualifying 1	Burscough	0	Clitheroe	2
Qualifying 1	Bury Town	2	Barton Rovers	0
Qualifying 1	Buxton	1	Stocksbridge Park Steels	2
Qualifying 1	Cambridge City	1	Aveley	0
Qualifying 1	Cammell Laird	1	Witton Albion	2
Qualifying 1	Canvey Island	1	AFC Sudbury	2
Qualifying 1	Carlton Town	1	Rushall Olympic	1
Qualifying 1	Carshalton Athletic	2	Ilford	0
Qualifying 1	Chesham United	1	Salisbury City	1
Qualifying 1	Chorley	1	Quorn	0
Qualifying 1	Cinderford Town	2	Hungerford Town	2
Qualifying 1	Cirencester Town	3	Halesowen Town	0
Qualifying 1	Colwyn Bay	2	Bradford Park Avenue	0
Qualifying 1	Cray Wanderers	2	Wingate & Finchley	1
Qualifying 1	Curzon Ashton	3	Skelmersdale United	1
Qualifying 1	Dulwich Hamlet	2	Hastings United	2
Qualifying 1	Durham City	0	FC Halifax Town	2
Qualifying 1	Enfield Town	2	Walton Casuals	1
Qualifying 1	Evesham United	1	Frome Town	0
Qualifying 1	FC United of Manchester	5	Newcastle Town	0
Qualifying 1	Faversham Town	1	Kingstonian	2
Qualifying 1	Fleet Town	0	Godalming Town	2
Qualifying 1	Folkestone Invicta	4	Worthing	2
Qualifying 1	Glapwell	2	Stamford	0
Qualifying 1	Great Wakering Rovers	1	Thamesmead Town	2
Qualifying 1	Harlow Town	3	Bedford Town	2
Qualifying 1	Harrogate Railway Athletic	2	Ossett Albion	1
Qualifying 1	Harrow Borough	0	Hendon	1
Qualifying 1	Hednesford Town	1	Whitby Town	2
Qualifying 1	Hemel Hempstead Town	2	Rugby Town	3
Qualifying 1	Horsham	3	Redbridge	0
Qualifying 1	Kendal Town	3	Frickley Athletic	0
Qualifying 1	Lancaster City	4	Ossett Town	2
Qualifying 1	Maidstone United	2	Burgess Hill Town	0
Qualifying 1	Margate	5	Whitehawk	1
Qualifying 1	Marine	2	Ashton United	2
Qualifying 1	Matlock Town	10	Bedworth United	0
Qualifying 1	Mickleover Sports	2	Hucknall Town	1

Qualifying 1	Market Drayton Town	1	Worksop Town	1	
Qualifying 1	North Ferriby United	0	Bamber Bridge	2	
Qualifying 1	Nantwich Town	6	Prescot Cables	2	
Qualifying 1	Needham Market	2	Lowestoft Town	2	
Qualifying 1	Northwich Victoria	0	Lincoln United	0	
Qualifying 1	Oxford City	1	Daventry Town	4	
Qualifying 1	Paulton Rovers	3	North Leigh	3	
Qualifying 1	Radcliffe Borough	1	Garforth Town	1	
Qualifying 1	Retford United	2	Romulus	2	
Qualifying 1	Sheffield	1	Chasetown	1	
Qualifying 1	Shepshed Dynamo	1	Mossley	4	
Qualifying 1	Slough Town	1	Chippenham Town	1	
Qualifying 1	Soham Town Rangers	1	Grays Athletic	2	
Qualifying 1	Sutton United	3	Tooting & Mitcham United	1	
Qualifying 1	Swindon Supermarine	4	Beaconsfield SYCOB	2	
Qualifying 1	Tonbridge Angels	3	Concord Rangers	2	
Qualifying 1	Truro City	1	Bishop's Cleeve	0	
Qualifying 1	Uxbridge	4	Abingdon United	1	
Qualifying 1	Waltham Forest	0	Romford	2	
Qualifying 1	Wealdstone	2	Potters Bar Town	2	
Qualifying 1	Weymouth	2	Bashley	1	
Qualifying 1	Windsor & Eton	1	Aylesbury	1	
Qualifying 1	Woodford United	1	Leamington	3	
Replay	Ashton United	1	Marine	3	
Replay	Aylesbury	1	Windsor & Eton	2	
Replay	Brackley Town	4	Burnham	0	
Replay	Chasetown	3	Sheffield	1	
Replay	Chippenham Town	4	Slough Town	1	
Replay	Garforth Town	1	Radcliffe Borough	2	
Replay	Hastings United	1	Dulwich Hamlet	2	
Replay	Hungerford Town	1	Cinderford Town	2	(aet)
Replay	Lincoln United	2	Northwich Victoria	3	
Replay	Lowestoft Town	6	Needham Market	2	
Replay	North Leigh	1	Paulton Rovers	2	
Replay	Potters Bar Town	1	Wealdstone	3	
Replay	Ramsgate	2	Arlesey Town	3	(aet)
Replay	Romulus	2	Retford United	1	
Replay	Rushall Olympic	4	Carlton Town	1	
Replay	Salisbury City	2	Chesham United	1	
Replay	Wimborne Town	1	Banbury United	3	(aet)
Replay	Worksop Town	1	Market Drayton Town	0	
Qualifying 2	AFC Sudbury	5	Hendon	1	
Qualifying 2	AFC Totton	1	Romford	3	
Qualifying 2	Arlesey Town	2	Uxbridge	2	
Qualifying 2	Ashford Town (Middlesex)	2	Bury Town	1	
Qualifying 2	Bideford	1	Dulwich Hamlet	0	
Qualifying 2	Billericay Town	2	Banbury United	1	
Qualifying 2	Bognor Regis Town	1	Godalming Town	1	
Qualifying 2	Brackley Town	4	Windsor & Eton	0	
Qualifying 2	Chippenham Town	1	Lowestoft Town	1	
Qualifying 2	Chorley	3	Marine	1	

Qualifying 2	Cirencester Town	2	Weymouth	1	
Qualifying 2	Cray Wanderers	1	Maidstone United	2	
Qualifying 2	Curzon Ashton	2	FC Halifax Town	1	
Qualifying 2	Daventry Town	1	Cambridge City	2	
Qualifying 2	Evesham United	0	Sutton United	1	
Qualifying 2	FC United of Manchester	2	Colwyn Bay	1	
Qualifying 2	Folkestone Invicta	0	Thamesmead Town	0	
Qualifying 2	Grays Athletic	2	Cinderford Town	1	
Qualifying 2	Harlow Town	2	Carshalton Athletic	0	
Qualifying 2	Kendal Town	1	Matlock Town	1	
Qualifying 2	Kingstonian	3	Wealdstone	5	
Qualifying 2	Leamington	3	Bamber Bridge	0	
Qualifying 2	Lowestoft Town	3	Chippenham Town	1	(aet)
Qualifying 2	Margate	1	AFC Hornchurch	2	
Qualifying 2	Mickleover Sports	2	Chasetown	5	
Qualifying 2	Mossley	2	Nantwich Town	3	
Qualifying 2	Northwich Victoria	4	Glapwell	0	
Qualifying 2	Paulton Rovers	4	Swindon Supermarine	5	
Qualifying 2	Radcliffe Borough	1	Witton Albion	1	
Qualifying 2	Romulus	1	Harrogate Railway Athletic	2	
Qualifying 2	Rushall Olympic	0	Stourbridge	1	
Qualifying 2	Salisbury City	2	Almondsbury Town	1	
Qualifying 2	Stocksbridge Park Steels	3	Rugby Town	2	
Qualifying 2	Tonbridge Angels	2	Enfield Town	0	
Qualifying 2	Truro City	2	Horsham	0	
Qualifying 2	Whitby Town	3	Clitheroe	1	
Qualifying 2	Worksop Town	2	Lancaster City	1	
Replay	Godalming Town	2	Bognor Regis Town	5	
Replay	Matlock Town	1	Kendal Town	2	
Replay	Thamesmead Town	1	Folkestone Invicta	3	
Replay	Uxbridge	4	Arlesey Town	2	
Replay	Witton Albion	3	Radcliffe Borough	1	
Qualifying 3	AFC Telford United	2	Corby Town	1	
Qualifying 3	Alfreton Town	4	Kendal Town	0	
Qualifying 3	Basingstoke Town	2	Havant & Waterlooville	2	
Qualifying 3	Bideford	0	AFC Hornchurch	3	
Qualifying 3	Blyth Spartans	1	Stafford Rangers	0	
Qualifying 3	Bognor Regis Town	2	Hampton & Richmond Borough	2	
Qualifying 3	Boreham Wood	3	Romford	0	
Qualifying 3	Boston United	2	Gainsborough Trinity	1	
Qualifying 3	Brackley Town	0	Wealdstone	1	
Qualifying 3	Braintree Town	2	Farnborough	0	
Qualifying 3	Bishop's Stortford	1	Ashford Town (Middlesex)	2	
Qualifying 3	Chorley	0	Guiseley	1	
Qualifying 3	Cirencester Town	2	Grays Athletic	2	
Qualifying 3	Curzon Ashton	2	Solihull Moors	1	
Qualifying 3	Dover Athletic	1	Woking	2	
Qualifying 3	Droylsden	3	Stourbridge	2	
Qualifying 3	Eastleigh	2	Folkestone Invicta	1	
Qualifying 3	Eastwood Town	2	Cambridge City	0	
Qualifying 3	Ebbsfleet United	4	Bromley	0	

Qualifying 3	FC United of Manchester	1	Hinckley United	2
Qualifying 3	Harlow Town	3	Maidstone United	0
Qualifying 3	Harrogate Railway Athletic	3	Nantwich Town	4
Qualifying 3	Harrogate Town	1	Witton Albion	1
Qualifying 3	Leamington	1	Hyde	2
Qualifying 3	Lewes	1	Salisbury City	3
Qualifying 3	Lowestoft Town	2	Swindon Supermarine	1
Qualifying 3	Maidenhead United	2	Uxbridge	4
Qualifying 3	Nuneaton Town	1	Worcester City	2
Qualifying 3	Redditch United	80	Bye	0
Qualifying 3	St. Albans City	3	Staines Town	1
Qualifying 3	Sutton United	4	Billericay Town	2
Qualifying 3	Thurrock	0	Dartford	2
Qualifying 3	Truro City	1	AFC Sudbury	2
Qualifying 3	Vauxhall Motors (Cheshire)	1	Stalybridge Celtic	3
Qualifying 3	Welling United	1	Tonbridge Angels	0
Qualifying 3	Weston-Super-Mare	1	Dorchester Town	3
Qualifying 3	Whitby Town	2	Northwich Victoria	2
Qualifying 3	Workington	0	Chasetown	0
Qualifying 3	Worksop Town	1	Chelmsford City	0
Qualifying 3	Worksop Town	4	Stocksbridge Park Steels	1
Replay	Chasetown	4	Workington	0
Replay	Grays Athletic	0	Cirencester Town	1
Replay	Hampton & Richmond Borough	2	Bognor Regis Town	0
Replay	Havant & Waterlooville	1	Basingstoke Town	2
Replay	Northwich Victoria	1	Whitby Town	0
Replay	Witton Albion	1	Harrogate Town	2
Round 1	AFC Sudbury	1	Hampton & Richmond Borough	4
Round 1	AFC Wimbledon	3	Braintree Town	0
Round 1	Alfreton Town	3	Hyde	0
Round 1	Ashford Town (Middlesex)	1	AFC Hornchurch	0
Round 1	Barrow	2	Guiseley	3
Round 1	Basingstoke Town	0	Salisbury City	2
Round 1	Blyth Spartans	2	Fleetwood Town	0
Round 1	Cambridge United	2	Forest Green Rovers	1
Round 1	Chasetown	3	Kettering Town	3
Round 1	Cirencester Town	1	Gloucester City	1
Round 1	Crawley Town	3	Dartford	3
Round 1	Curzon Ashton	2	Altrincham	1
	The match was abandoned at half-time due to power failure and a replay was ordered.			
Round 1	Darlington	3	Tamworth	2
Round 1	Dorchester Town	3	St. Albans City	0
Round 1	Droylsden	4	Hinckley United	3
Round 1	Eastbourne Borough	3	Boreham Wood	1
Round 1	Eastleigh	1	Sutton United	1
Round 1	Ebbsfleet United	3	Hayes & Yeading United	1
Round 1	Gateshead	2	Southport	2
Round 1	Grimsby Town	3	Redditch United	0
Round 1	Harlow Town	0	Woking	2
Round 1	Harrogate Town	0	AFC Telford United	3
Round 1	Histon	2	Bath City	3

Round 1	Lowestoft Town	2	Uxbridge	3	
Round 1	Luton Town	0	Welling United	0	
Round 1	Newport County	0	Wealdstone	0	
Round 1	Rushden & Diamonds	1	Eastwood Town	1	
Round 1	Stalybridge Celtic	2	Nantwich Town	1	
Round 1	Worcester City	1	Northwich Victoria	0	
Round 1	Worksop Town	0	Mansfield Town	5	
	Match played at Retford				
Round 1	Wrexham	2	Kidderminster Harriers	0	
Round 1	York City	0	Boston United	1	
Replay	Curzon Ashton	0	Altrincham	2	
Replay	Dartford	1	Crawley Town	0	
Replay	Eastwood Town	4	Rushden & Diamonds	3	(aet)
Replay	Gloucester City	3	Cirencester Town	0	
Replay	Kettering Town	1	Chasetown	2	(aet)
Replay	Southport	0	Gateshead	1	
Replay	Sutton United	0	Eastleigh	4	
Replay	Wealdstone	0	Newport County	1	(aet)
Replay	Welling United	1	Luton Town	2	
Round 2	AFC Telford United	1	Eastwood Town	0	
Round 2	AFC Wimbledon	2	Woking	3	
Round 2	Alfreton Town	3	Cambridge United	3	
Round 2	Ashford Town (Middlesex)	0	Dartford	1	
Round 2	Blyth Spartans	2	Altrincham	1	
Round 2	Boston United	0	Gloucester City	1	
Round 2	Chasetown	2	Grimsby Town	1	
Round 2	Darlington	4	Bath City	1	
Round 2	Dorchester Town	3	Eastbourne Borough	3	
Round 2	Droylsden	1	Ebbsfleet United	0	
Round 2	Eastleigh	3	Worcester City	3	
Round 2	Gateshead	6	Hampton & Richmond Borough	0	
Round 2	Guiseley	2	Stalybridge Celtic	1	
Round 2	Luton Town	4	Uxbridge	0	
Round 2	Mansfield Town	4	Newport County	2	
Round 2	Salisbury City	1	Wrexham	0	
Replay	Cambridge United	3	Alfreton Town	6	(aet)
Replay	Eastbourne Borough	1	Dorchester Town	0	
Replay	Worcester City	1	Eastleigh	4	
Round 3	AFC Telford United	0	Darlington	3	
Round 3	Blyth Spartans	2	Droylsden	2	
Round 3	Eastbourne Borough	1	Guiseley	1	
Round 3	Eastleigh	1	Chasetown	3	
Round 3	Gateshead	3	Dartford	0	
Round 3	Luton Town	1	Gloucester City	0	
Round 3	Mansfield Town	1	Alfreton Town	1	
Round 3	Woking	0	Salisbury City	2	
Replay	Alfreton Town	1	Mansfield Town	2	
Replay	Droylsden	0	Blyth Spartans	4	
Replay	Guiseley	2	Eastbourne Borough	1	

Round 4	Blyth Spartans	0	Gateshead	2	
Round 4	Chasetown	2	Mansfield Town	2	
Round 4	Darlington	2	Salisbury City	1	
Round 4	Guiseley	0	Luton Town	1	
Replay	Mansfield Town	3	Chasetown	1	
Semi-finals					
1st leg	Darlington	3	Gateshead	2	
2nd leg	Gateshead	0	Darlington	0	
	Darlington won 3-2 on aggregate.				
1st leg	Mansfield Town	1	Luton Town	0	
2nd leg	Luton Town	1	Mansfield Town	1	(aet)
	Mansfield Town won 2-1 on aggregate				
FINAL	Darlington	1	Mansfield Town	0	

Cup Statistics provided by:

www.soccerdata.com

F.A. Vase 2010/2011

Round	Home	Score	Away	Score	
Round 1	AFC Dunstable	3	Colney Heath	1	
Round 1	AFC Emley	3	Runcorn Linnets	1	
Round 1	AFC Liverpool	3	Hallam	0	
Round 1	Atherton Laburnum Rovers	2	Runcorn Town	3	
Round 1	Aylesbury United	4	Hertford Town	3	(aet)
Round 1	Baldock Town Letchworth	0	Holyport	1	
Round 1	Barking	1	Flackwell Heath	2	
Round 1	Bedlington Terriers	0	Spennymoor Town	1	
Round 1	Bemerton Heath Harlequins	5	Lydney Town	2	(aet)
Round 1	Billingham Town	3	Ashington	4	(aet)
Round 1	Binfield	3	Hillingdon Borough	2	
Round 1	Bishop Auckland	3	Billingham Synthonia	4	(aet)
Round 1	Bishop Sutton	2	Keynsham Town	2	(aet)
Round 1	Blaby & Whetstone Athletic	2	Westfields	5	
Round 1	Bloxwich United	5	Pilkington XXX	0	
Round 1	Boldmere St. Michaels	1	Continental Star	0	
Round 1	Bookham	0	Herne Bay	4	
Round 1	Bracknell Town	2	Wodson Park	0	
Round 1	Brading Town	4	St. Francis Rangers	2	
Round 1	Brighouse Town	3	Eccleshill United	3	(aet)
Round 1	Brislington	0	St. Blazey	1	
Round 1	Burnham Ramblers	2	Kentish Town	0	(aet)
Round 1	Cadbury Heath	2	Wootton Bassett Town	1	
Round 1	Calne Town	1	Downton	2	
Round 1	Camberley Town	2	Blackfield & Langley	1	
Round 1	Cambridge Regional College	4	Wellingborough Town	0	
Round 1	Chalfont St. Peter	6	Newbury (2)	0	
Round 1	Clanfield 85	2	Fairford Town	1	
Round 1	Coalville Town	2	Stratford Town	1	
Round 1	Cockfosters	0	Witham Town	3	
Round 1	Colliers Wood United	5	Cove	2	
Round 1	Corinthian	0	Tunbridge Wells	4	
Round 1	Coventry Copsewood	2	Heath Town Rangers	1	
Round 1	Coventry Sphinx	4	Anstey Nomads	3	
Round 1	Crawley Down	0	Rye United	1	
Round 1	Croydon	3	Beckenham Town	7	
Round 1	Dunkirk	2	Blidworth Welfare	0	
Round 1	Dunstable Town	5	AFC Wallingford	0	
Round 1	Dunston UTS	2	Washington	1	
Round 1	Eccleshall	2	Bridgnorth Town	4	
Round 1	Egham Town	2	Molesey	0	
Round 1	Erith & Belvedere	2	Chichester City	1	(aet)
Round 1	Eton Manor	4	FC Clacton	2	
Round 1	Fisher	1	Warlingham	3	
Round 1	Forest Town	3	Greenwood Meadows	1	
Round 1	Formby	2	Flixton	0	
Round 1	Gedling Town	2	Glossop North End	1	
Round 1	Godmanchester Rovers	4	Framlingham Town	0	
Round 1	Gorleston	1	Hadleigh United	0	

Round 1	Guildford City (2)	3	Horley Town	2	(aet)
Round 1	Haringey Borough	1	Tring Athletic	3	
Round 1	Heanor Town	6	Clipstone Welfare	2	
Round 1	Holbrook Sports	4	Arnold Town	4	(aet)
Round 1	Holwell Sports	4	Tividale	3	
Round 1	Ilfracombe Town	1	Hengrove Athletic	2	
Round 1	Ipswich Wanderers	1	Walsham Le Willows	2	
Round 1	Irlam	2	Colne	0	
Round 1	Kidlington	0	Bitton	1	
Round 1	Lancing	1	Christchurch	1	(aet)
Round 1	Langford	1	Hullbridge Sports	3	
Round 1	Leeds Carnegie	4	Easington Colliery	0	
Round 1	Leiston	3	Haverhill Rovers	2	(aet)
Round 1	Leverstock Green	5	Enfield 1893	4	
Round 1	Lordswood	1	Three Bridges	2	
Round 1	Louth Town	3	Barton Town Old Boys	3	
Round 1	Lymington Town	1	Bournemouth (Ams)	2	
Round 1	Maine Road	2	AFC Blackpool	2	(aet)
Round 1	Malvern Town	2	Heather St. Johns	6	
Round 1	Melksham Town	3	Laverstock & Ford	1	
Round 1	Moneyfields	1	Greenwich Borough	0	
Round 1	Newport (IOW)	3	Shoreham	0	
Round 1	Northallerton Town	3	Stokesley	4	
Round 1	Odd Down	7	Bridport	0	
Round 1	Peacehaven & Telscombe	1	Hamble ASSC	0	
Round 1	Ramsbottom United	0	Staveley Miners Welfare	1	
Round 1	Raynes Park Vale	0	Hythe Town	3	
Round 1	Reading Town	4	Newport Pagnell Town	2	
Round 1	Rossendale United	0	Bacup Borough	2	
Round 1	Saltash United	9	Newquay	1	
Round 1	Scarborough Athletic	2	Bridlington Town	2	(aet)
Round 1	Sherborne Town	2	Bodmin Town	2	(aet)
Round 1	South Shields	0	Thackley	2	
Round 1	St. Helens Town	2	Oldham Boro	1	
	Match played at Ashton Town FC				
Round 1	St. Neots Town	11	Felixstowe & Walton United	0	
Round 1	Stansted	2	Takeley	0	
Round 1	Stanway Rovers	4	London APSA	0	
Round 1	Stone Dominoes	1	Heath Hayes	4	
Round 1	Tadcaster Albion	2	Tow Law Town	0	
Round 1	Thrapston Town	2	King's Lynn Town	4	
Round 1	Thurnby Nirvana	1	Shifnal Town	2	
Round 1	Torpoint Athletic	4	Radstock Town	1	
Round 1	Verwood Town	1	Budleigh Salterton	0	(aet)
Round 1	Wantage Town	2	Shrivenham	1	
Round 1	Wednesfield	4	Studley	3	
Round 1	Wellington	5	Tavistock	0	
Round 1	West Auckland Town	6	Birtley Town	0	
Round 1	Whitton United	2	Norwich United	0	
Round 1	Wick	0	VCD Athletic	2	(aet)
Round 1	Willenhall Town	0	Gornal Athletic	2	
Round 1	Winterton Rangers	3	Deeping Rangers	1	

Round 1	Wisbech Town	5	Cogenhoe United	1	
Round 1	Wolverhampton Casuals	1	Bustleholme	3	
Replay	AFC Blackpool	2	Maine Road	1	
Replay	Arnold Town	1	Holbrook Sports	3	
Replay	Barton Town Old Boys	1	Louth Town	0	(aet)
Replay	Bodmin Town	1	Sherborne Town	0	
Replay	Bridlington Town	1	Scarborough Athletic	3	
Replay	Christchurch	0	Lancing	1	
Replay	Eccleshill United	2	Brighouse Town	1	
Replay	Keynsham Town	1	Bishop Sutton	0	
Round 2	AFC Blackpool	0	AFC Liverpool	2	
Round 2	AFC Dunstable	1	Tring Athletic	2	
Round 2	Beckenham Town	2	Peacehaven & Telscombe	1	(aet)
Round 2	Billingham Synthonia	3	Stokesley	1	
Round 2	Bitton	2	Shortwood United	1	
Round 2	Boldmere St. Michaels	1	Gornal Athletic	2	
Round 2	Bootle	1	Shildon	3	
Round 2	Bournemouth (Ams)	5	Odd Down	0	
Round 2	Bridgnorth Town	2	Coalville Town	4	
Round 2	Bristol Manor Farm	3	Torpoint Athletic	7	
Round 2	Bustleholme	2	Barton Town Old Boys	0	
Round 2	Causeway United	2	Gedling Town	0	
Round 2	Chertsey Town	1	Moneyfields	2	
Round 2	Clanfield 85	0	Bemerton Heath Harlequins	3	
Round 2	Colliers Wood United	1	Witney United	0	
	Played at Croydon FC				
Round 2	Coventry Sphinx	0	Dunkirk	3	
Round 2	Dawlish Town	0	Bodmin Town	2	
Round 2	Downton	2	Cadbury Heath	3	
Round 2	Dunstable Town	2	Cambridge Regional College	1	
Round 2	Dunston UTS	4	AFC Emley	0	
Round 2	Eccleshill United	0	Runcorn Town	2	
Round 2	Egham Town	1	Newport (IOW)	2	
Round 2	Epsom & Ewell	4	Bracknell Town	0	
Round 2	Erith & Belvedere	0	Lancing	2	
Round 2	Flackwell Heath	1	Three Bridges	2	
Round 2	Forest Town	0	Tadcaster Albion	4	
Round 2	Formby	1	Bacup Borough	0	
Round 2	Godmanchester Rovers	0	Stanway Rovers	1	
Round 2	Gresley	2	Heanor Town	0	
Round 2	Guildford City	5	Brading Town	2	
Round 2	Heath Hayes	2	Tipton Town	1	
Round 2	Herne Bay	3	Camberley Town	0	
Round 2	Holbrook Sports	7	Holwell Sports	0	
Round 2	Hullbridge Sports	1	Leverstock Green	5	
Round 2	King's Lynn Town	4	Gorleston	0	
Round 2	Kirkley & Pakefield	0	Long Buckby	1	
Round 2	Leeds Carnegie	4	Marske United	3	(aet)
Round 2	New Mills	2	Ashington	4	
Round 2	Norton & Stockton Ancients	4	Irlam	3	
Round 2	Plymouth Parkway	6	Melksham Town	1	

Round	Home	Score	Away	Score	
Round 2	Poole Town	4	Wellington	3	
Round 2	Reading Town	1	Warlingham	0	
Round 2	Royston Town	2	Leiston	2	(aet)
Round 2	Rye United	4	Chalfont St. Peter	4	(aet)
	Match played at Sussex County Ground, Lancing				
Round 2	Scarborough Athletic	2	Armthorpe Welfare	2	(aet)
Round 2	Shifnal Town	2	Bloxwich United	2	(aet)
Round 2	St. Blazey	1	Hengrove Athletic	1	(aet)
Round 2	St. Ives Town	2	Aylesbury United	1	
Round 2	St. Neots Town	6	Burnham Ramblers	1	
Round 2	Stansted	3	Eton Manor	1	
Round 2	Staveley Miners Welfare	1	Pickering Town	0	(aet)
Round 2	Stotfold	2	Whitton United	1	
Round 2	Thackley	0	Whitley Bay	1	
Round 2	Tunbridge Wells	8	Holyport	0	
Round 2	VCD Athletic	1	Hythe Town	5	
Round 2	Verwood Town	2	Keynsham Town	1	
Round 2	Wantage Town	3	Binfield	1	
Round 2	Wednesfield	1	Heather St. Johns	3	(aet)
Round 2	West Auckland Town	1	Spennymoor Town	3	
Round 2	Westfields	3	Coventry Copsewood	0	
Round 2	Willand Rovers	2	Saltash United	1	
Round 2	Winterton Rangers	0	St. Helens Town	2	
Round 2	Witham Town	3	Walsham Le Willows	1	
Round 2	Wroxham	4	Wisbech Town	0	
Replay	Armthorpe Welfare	2	Scarborough Athletic	3	
Replay	Bloxwich United	5	Shifnal Town	3	
Replay	Chalfont St. Peter	1	Rye United	2	
Replay	Hengrove Athletic	0	St. Blazey	2	
Replay	Leiston	1	Royston Town	0	
Round 3	Beckenham Town	1	King's Lynn Town	2	
Round 3	Bitton	4	Newport (IOW)	1	
Round 3	Cadbury Heath	4	Reading Town	1	
Round 3	Causeway United	0	Norton & Stockton Ancients	3	
Round 3	Dunkirk	1	Ashington	2	
Round 3	Dunston UTS	2	Heather St. Johns	0	
Round 3	Epsom & Ewell	1	St. Neots Town	2	
Round 3	Formby	2	Tadcaster Albion	3	
Round 3	Gornal Athletic	0	Runcorn Town	3	
Round 3	Gresley	4	Bustleholme	2	
Round 3	Guildford City	4	Moneyfields	3	
Round 3	Heath Hayes	1	Bloxwich United	3	
Round 3	Herne Bay	2	Colliers Wood United	0	
Round 3	Holbrook Sports	4	St. Helens Town	0	
Round 3	Lancing	4	Witham Town	2	(aet)
Round 3	Leeds Carnegie	1	Staveley Miners Welfare	4	
Round 3	Leiston	3	Hythe Town	1	
Round 3	Leverstock Green	3	Tunbridge Wells	1	
Round 3	Plymouth Parkway	1	Bodmin Town	3	(aet)
Round 3	Poole Town	3	Wantage Town	2	
Round 3	Scarborough Athletic	0	Spennymoor Town	3	

Round 3	Shildon	0	Coalville Town	2	
Round 3	St. Blazey	1	Bemerton Heath Harlequins	2	
Round 3	Stanway Rovers	0	Stansted	1	
Round 3	Stotfold	0	Long Buckby	3	
Round 3	Three Bridges	1	Rye United	3	(aet)
Round 3	Tring Athletic	1	Dunstable Town	6	
Round 3	Verwood Town	2	Torpoint Athletic	5	
Round 3	Westfields	1	Billingham Synthonia	2	(aet)
Round 3	Whitley Bay	7	AFC Liverpool	1	
Round 3	Willand Rovers	2	Bournemouth (Ams)	1	
Round 3	Wroxham	0	St. Ives Town	1	(aet)
Round 4	Billingham Synthonia	2	Tadcaster Albion	1	
Round 4	Bitton	2	Coalville Town	3	
Round 4	Bloxwich United	2	Torpoint Athletic	3	
Round 4	Bodmin Town	1	Stansted	4	
Round 4	Cadbury Heath	1	Spennymoor Town	5	
Round 4	Dunstable Town	2	Willand Rovers	0	
Round 4	Gresley	1	St. Neots Town	3	
Round 4	Guildford City	2	Leiston	6	(aet)
Round 4	Herne Bay	1	Whitley Bay	2	
Round 4	Holbrook Sports	2	Lancing	1	
Round 4	Leverstock Green	4	Bemerton Heath Harlequins	1	
Round 4	Long Buckby	3	Ashington	2	
Round 4	Norton & Stockton Ancients	0	King's Lynn Town	1	
Round 4	Poole Town	3	St. Ives Town	2	
Round 4	Runcorn Town	1	Dunston UTS	3	
Round 4	Staveley Miners Welfare	0	Rye United	3	
Round 5	Coalville Town	3	Holbrook Sports	1	(aet)
Round 5	King's Lynn Town	2	St. Neots Town	1	
Round 5	Leiston	2	Long Buckby	1	
Round 5	Leverstock Green	1	Rye United	2	
Round 5	Poole Town	3	Spennymoor Town	2	
Round 5	Stansted	0	Dunston UTS	2	
Round 5	Torpoint Athletic	1	Billingham Synthonia	0	
Round 5	Whitley Bay	5	Dunstable Town	1	
Round 6	Coalville Town	1	Leiston	0	
Round 6	Dunston UTS	1	Whitley Bay	2	
Round 6	King's Lynn Town	3	Rye United	1	(aet)
Round 6	Poole Town	2	Torpoint Athletic	1	
Semi-finals					
1st leg	Coalville Town	3	King's Lynn Town	0	
2nd leg	King's Lynn Town	2	Coalville Town	3	
	Coalville Town won 6-2 on aggregate				
1st leg	Poole Town	1	Whitley Bay	2	
2nd leg	Whitley Bay	3	Poole Town	1	
	Whitley Bay won 5-2 on aggregate				
FINAL	Whitley Bay	3	Coalville Town	2	

ENGLAND INTERNATIONAL LINE-UPS AND STATISTICS 2010

18th June 2010
v ALGERIA (WCF)   *Cape Town*
D. James	Portsmouth
G. Johnson	Liverpool
A. Cole	Chelsea
S. Gerrard	Liverpool
J. Carragher	Liverpool
J. Terry	Chelsea
A. Lennon	Tottenham H. (sub. S. Wright-Phillips 63)
F. Lampard	Chelsea
E. Heskey	Aston Villa (sub. J. Defoe 74)
W. Rooney	Manchester United
G. Barry	Manchester City (sub. P. Crouch 84)

Result 0-0

23rd June 2010
v SLOVAKIA (WCF)   *Port Elizabeth*
D. James	Portsmouth
G. Johnson	Liverpool
A. Cole	Chelsea
S. Gerrard	Liverpool
M. Upson	West Ham United
J. Terry	Chelsea
J. Milner	Aston Villa
F. Lampard	Chelsea
J. Defoe	Tottenham H. (sub. E. Heskey 86)
W. Rooney	Manchester United (sub. J. Cole 72)
G. Barry	Manchester City

Result 1-0   Defoe

27th June 2010
v GERMANY (WCF)   *Bloemfontein*
D. James	Portsmouth
G. Johnson	Liverpool (sub. S. Wright-Phillips 87)
A. Cole	Chelsea
S. Gerrard	Liverpool
M. Upson	West Ham United
J. Terry	Chelsea
J. Milner	Aston Villa (sub. J. Cole 63)
F. Lampard	Chelsea
J. Defoe	Tottenham H. (sub. E. Heskey 71)
W. Rooney	Manchester United
G. Barry	Manchester City

Result 1-4   Upson

11th August 2010
v HUNGARY   *Wembley*
J. Hart	Manchester City
G. Johnson	Liverpool
A. Cole	Chelsea (sub. K. Gibbs 46)
S. Gerrard	Liverpool (sub. J. Wilshire 82)
P. Jagielka	Everton
J. Terry	Chelsea (sub. M. Dawson 46)
T. Walcott	Arsenal (sub. B. Zamora 46)
F. Lampard	Chelsea (sub. A. Young 46)
A. Johnson	Manchester City
W. Rooney	Manchester Utd. (sub. J. Milner 66)
G. Barry	Manchester City

Result 2-1   Gerrard 2

3rd September 2010
v BULGARIA (ECQ)   *Wembley*
J. Hart	Manchester City
G. Johnson	Liverpool
A. Cole	Chelsea
S. Gerrard	Liverpool
M. Dawson	Tottenham Hotspur (sub. G. Cahill 57)
P. Jagielka	Everton
T. Walcott	Arsenal (sub. A. Johnson 74)
G. Barry	Manchester City
J. Defoe	Tottenham Hotspur (sub. A. Young 87)
W. Rooney	Manchester United
J. Milner	Manchester City

Result 4-0   Defoe 3, Johnson

7th September 2010
v SWITZERLAND (ECQ)   *Basle*
J. Hart	Manchester City
G. Johnson	Liverpool
A. Cole	Chelsea
S. Gerrard	Liverpool
J. Lescott	Manchester City
P. Jagielka	Everton
T. Walcott	Arsenal (sub. A. Johnson 13)
G. Barry	Manchester City
J. Defoe	Tottenham Hotspur (sub. D. Bent 70)
W. Rooney	Man. Utd. (sub. S. Wright-Phillips 79)
J. Milner	Manchester City

Result 3-1   Rooney, Johnson, Bent

ENGLAND INTERNATIONAL LINE-UPS AND STATISTICS 2010-2011

12th October 2010
v MONTENEGRO (ECQ) *Wembley*
J. Hart   Manchester City
G. Johnson   Liverpool
A. Cole   Chelsea
S. Gerrard   Liverpool
R. Ferdinand   Manchester United
J. Lescott   Manchester City
A. Young   Aston Villa (sub. S. Wright-Phillips 74)
G. Barry   Manchester City
P. Crouch   Tottenham Hotspur (sub. K. Davies 69)
W. Rooney   Manchester United
A. Johnson   Manchester City
Result 0-0

17th November 2010
v FRANCE *Wembley*
B. Foster   Birmingham City
P. Jagielka   Everton
K. Gibbs   Arsenal (sub. S. Warnock 72)
S. Gerrard   Liverpool (sub. P. Crouch 84)
R. Ferdinand   Man. United (sub. M. Richards 46)
J. Lescott   Manchester City
T. Walcott   Arsenal (sub. A. Johnson 46)
J. Henderson   Sunderland
A. Caroll   Newcastle Utd. (sub. J. Bothroyd 72)
G. Barry   Manchester City (sub. A. Young 46)
J. Milner   Manchester City
Result 1-2 Crouch

9th February 2011
v DENMARK *Copenhagen*
J. Hart   Manchester City
G. Johnson   Liverpool
A. Cole   Chelsea (sub. L. Baines 81)
J. Wilshere   Arsenal (sub. G. Barry 46)
M. Dawson   Tottenham Hotspur (sub. G. Cahill 60)
J. Terry   Chelsea
T. Walcott   Arsenal (sub. S. Downing 67)
F. Lampard   Chelsea (sub. S. Parker 46)
D. Bent   Aston Villa
W. Rooney   Manchester Utd. (sub. A. Young 46)
J. Milner   Manchester City
Result 2-1 Bent, Young

26th March 2011
v WALES (ECQ) *Cardiff*
J. Hart   Manchester City
G. Johnson   Liverpool
A. Cole   Chelsea
S. Parker   West Ham Utd. (sub. P. Jagielka 88)
M. Dawson   Tottenham Hotspur
J. Terry   Chelsea
F. Lampard   Chelsea
J. Wilshere   Arsenal (sub. S. Downing 82)
D. Bent   Aston Villa
W. Rooney   Manchester Utd. (sub. J. Milner 70)
A. Young   Aston Villa
Result 2-0 Lampard (pen), Bent

29th March 2011
v GHANA *Wembley*
J. Hart   Manchester City
G. Johnson   Liverpool (sub. J. Lescott 46)
L. Baines   Everton
G. Barry   Manchester City
G. Cahill   Bolton Wanderers
P. Jagielka   Everton
J. Milner   Manchester City
J. Wilshere   Arsenal (sub. M. Jarvis 69)
A. Caroll   Liverpool (sub. J. Defoe 59)
A. Young   Aston Villa (sub. D. Welbeck 81)
S. Downing   Aston Villa
Result 1-1 Carroll

4th June 2011
v SWITZERLAND (ECQ) *Wembley*
J. Hart   Manchester City
G. Johnson   Liverpool
A. Cole   Chelsea (sub. L Baines 30)
S. Parker   West Ham United
R. Ferdinand   Manchester United
J. Terry   Chelsea
T. Walcott   Arsenal (sub. S. Downing 77)
F. Lampard   Chelsea (sub. A. Young 46)
D. Bent   Aston Villa
J. Wilshere   Arsenal
J. Milner   Manchester City
Result 2-2 Lampard (pen), Young

Evo-Stik League Southern Premier Division 2011/2012 Fixtures

	AFC Totton	Arlesey Town	Banbury United	Barwell	Bashley	Bedford Town	Brackley Town	Cambridge City	Chesham United	Chippenham Town	Cirencester Town	Evesham United	Frome Town	Hemel Hempstead Town	Hitchin Town	Leamington	Oxford City	Redditch United	St. Albans City	Stourbridge	Swindon Supermarine	Weymouth
AFC Totton	■	14/04	12/11	03/09	26/12	28/04	14/01	15/10	07/01	07/04	04/10	18/02	03/03	10/12	24/09	24/03	16/08	17/03	04/02	26/11	20/08	29/08
Arlesey Town	13/08	■	03/03	04/10	24/09	21/01	23/08	29/08	07/04	19/11	12/11	17/03	03/12	04/02	26/12	17/12	15/10	21/04	18/02	24/03	10/09	07/01
Banbury United	10/03	15/21	■	17/12	03/12	31/12	09/04	11/02	13/09	25/02	19/11	14/01	31/03	03/09	13/08	21/04	02/01	23/08	27/08	28/01	29/10	08/10
Barwell	21/01	28/01	16/08	■	07/01	10/12	13/09	17/03	14/04	08/10	15/10	28/04	12/11	24/03	07/04	26/12	10/09	03/03	20/08	29/08	26/11	11/02
Bashley	09/04	11/02	20/08	31/03	■	26/11	10/03	10/09	15/11	13/09	31/12	14/04	28/01	28/04	21/01	25/02	10/12	27/08	29/10	08/10	02/01	16/08
Bedford Town	19/11	03/09	07/04	23/08	21/04	■	03/12	26/12	29/10	14/01	18/02	07/01	13/08	15/11	29/08	04/02	24/09	17/12	04/10	10/03	25/02	24/03
Brackley Town	10/09	10/12	26/12	04/02	12/11	20/08	■	03/03	16/08	24/03	24/09	29/08	21/01	07/04	15/10	18/02	26/11	11/10	28/04	07/01	14/04	17/03
Cambridge City	25/02	02/01	24/09	29/10	14/01	09/04	15/11	■	10/12	03/09	31/03	26/11	27/08	04/10	04/02	10/03	31/12	18/02	16/08	20/08	28/04	14/04
Chesham Town	31/03	31/12	04/02	13/08	03/03	17/03	17/12	23/08	■	03/12	02/01	24/09	21/04	18/02	04/10	19/11	12/11	15/10	09/04	21/01	27/08	10/09
Chippenham Town	31/12	28/04	15/10	18/02	04/02	10/09	27/08	21/01	20/08	■	03/03	16/08	02/01	24/09	17/03	04/10	31/03	12/11	26/11	14/04	09/04	10/12
Cirencester Town	28/01	10/03	28/04	25/02	07/04	08/10	11/02	07/01	29/08	15/11	■	26/12	10/09	26/11	24/03	29/10	20/08	21/01	14/04	16/08	10/12	13/09
Evesham United	08/10	29/10	10/09	19/11	13/08	31/03	02/01	21/04	11/02	17/12	09/04	■	23/08	25/02	04/02	15/11	27/08	31/12	10/03	13/09	28/01	21/01
Frome Town	16/11	20/08	07/01	10/03	12/10	14/04	03/09	24/03	26/11	29/08	14/01	10/12	■	29/10	18/02	07/04	04/02	24/09	25/02	28/04	17/08	26/12
Hemel Hempstead T.	23/08	13/09	21/01	27/08	19/11	03/03	31/12	28/01	08/10	11/02	21/04	15/10	17/03	■	17/12	13/08	09/04	03/12	02/01	10/09	31/03	12/11
Hitchin Town	11/02	09/04	14/04	31/12	03/09	02/01	25/02	12/09	28/01	29/10	27/08	20/08	08/10	15/08	■	14/01	28/04	31/03	10/12	14/11	10/03	26/11
Leamington	27/08	16/08	26/11	09/04	15/10	13/09	08/10	12/11	28/04	28/01	17/03	03/03	31/12	14/04	10/09	■	21/01	02/01	31/03	10/12	11/02	20/08
Oxford City	17/12	25/02	29/08	14/01	23/08	11/02	21/04	07/04	10/03	07/01	03/12	24/03	13/09	26/12	19/11	03/09	■	13/08	15/11	29/10	08/10	28/01
Redditch United	29/10	26/11	10/12	15/11	24/03	16/08	28/01	08/10	25/02	10/03	03/09	07/04	11/02	20/08	07/01	29/08	14/04	■	14/01	26/12	13/09	28/04
St. Albans City	13/09	08/10	24/03	03/12	17/03	28/01	19/11	17/12	26/12	21/04	13/08	12/11	15/10	29/08	23/08	07/01	03/03	10/09	■	11/02	21/01	07/04
Stourbridge	21/04	27/08	04/10	02/01	18/02	12/11	31/03	03/12	03/09	13/08	17/12	04/02	19/11	14/01	03/03	23/08	17/03	09/04	24/09	■	31/12	15/10
Swindon Supermar.	03/12	14/01	17/03	21/04	29/08	15/10	13/08	19/11	24/03	26/12	24/08	05/10	17/12	07/01	12/11	24/09	18/02	04/02	03/09	07/04	■	03/03
Weymouth	02/01	31/03	18/02	24/09	17/12	27/08	29/10	13/08	14/01	23/08	04/02	03/09	09/04	10/03	21/04	03/12	04/10	19/11	31/12	25/02	15/11	■

Evo-Stik League Southern Division One Central 2011/2012 Fixtures

	AFC Hayes	Ashford Town (Middlesex)	Aylesbury	Barton Rovers	Beaconsfield SYCOB	Bedfont Town	Bedworth United	Biggleswade Town	Burnham	Chalfont St. Peter	Chertsey Town	Daventry Town	Fleet Town	Leighton Town	Marlow	North Greenford United	Northwood	Rugby Town	Slough Town	St. Neots Town	Uxbridge	Woodford United
AFC Hayes	■	03/03	17/03	31/03	27/08	11/02	03/12	26/11	05/11	17/12	14/01	12/11	04/10	13/08	10/09	09/04	23/08	21/04	01/10	25/02	02/01	28/01
Ashford Town (Mx)	15/11	■	10/09	17/12	03/12	02/01	01/10	25/02	14/01	11/02	23/08	29/10	09/04	28/01	31/03	27/08	13/08	10/03	24/03	28/04	04/10	19/11
Aylesbury	19/11	15/10	■	04/02	02/01	27/08	15/11	31/03	24/09	09/04	10/03	16/08	24/03	13/09	17/12	05/11	18/02	07/01	21/01	20/08	03/12	21/04
Barton Rovers	10/12	14/04	04/10	■	28/01	13/08	14/01	10/09	17/03	25/02	28/04	07/04	01/10	26/12	29/10	12/11	31/12	11/02	29/08	03/03	23/08
Beaconsfield SYCOB	31/12	07/04	29/08	20/08	■	10/09	25/02	01/10	10/12	03/10	14/11	28/04	29/10	19/11	15/08	07/01	14/04	24/03	26/12	21/01	11/02	10/03
Bedfont Town	14/09	29/08	31/12	21/01	15/10	■	21/04	12/11	03/03	20/08	26/12	14/04	17/08	10/12	07/01	17/03	04/02	18/02	07/04	26/11	05/11	24/09
Bedworth United	07/04	18/02	03/03	16/08	24/09	29/10	■	28/04	26/11	21/01	10/12	29/08	20/08	04/02	17/03	15/10	31/12	26/12	14/04	07/01	12/11	13/09
Biggleswade Town	24/03	24/09	10/12	15/10	18/02	10/03	05/11	■	31/12	07/01	14/04	13/09	21/01	29/08	20/08	16/08	07/04	04/02	19/11	26/12	21/04	15/11
Burnham	28/04	15/08	25/02	19/11	31/03	14/11	24/03	27/08	■	02/01	03/10	21/01	11/02	10/03	09/04	03/12	29/10	20/08	07/01	01/10	10/09	17/12
Chalfont St. Peter	14/04	13/09	26/12	24/09	04/02	28/01	13/08	23/08	29/08	■	29/10	26/11	28/04	15/10	12/11	03/03	14/01	07/04	10/12	31/12	17/03	18/02
Chertsey Town	16/08	07/01	12/11	05/11	03/03	09/04	31/03	17/12	04/02	21/04	■	15/10	02/01	18/02	26/11	13/09	24/09	21/01	20/08	17/03	27/08	03/12
Daventry Town	10/03	21/04	14/01	03/12	05/11	17/12	02/01	11/02	13/08	24/03	10/09	■	19/11	23/08	27/08	31/03	28/01	15/11	25/02	11/10	01/10	09/04
Fleet Town	04/02	26/12	26/11	18/02	21/04	14/01	28/01	13/08	13/09	05/11	29/08	17/03	■	07/04	03/03	24/09	12/11	10/12	31/12	14/04	23/08	15/10
Leighton Town	21/01	20/08	11/02	09/04	17/03	31/03	04/10	02/01	12/11	10/09	01/10	07/01	03/12	■	25/02	26/11	28/04	16/08	29/10	03/03	17/12	27/08
Marlow	15/10	10/12	14/04	21/04	14/01	23/08	19/11	28/01	26/12	14/04	24/03	31/12	15/11	24/09	■	18/02	13/09	05/11	29/08	07/04	13/08	04/02
North Greenford Utd.	26/12	31/12	28/04	10/03	23/08	19/11	10/09	14/01	07/04	15/11	11/02	10/12	25/02	24/03	01/10	■	29/08	14/04	04/10	29/10	28/01	13/08
Northwood	07/01	21/01	01/10	24/03	17/12	04/10	27/08	03/12	21/04	16/08	25/02	20/08	10/03	05/11	11/02	02/01	■	19/11	15/11	10/09	09/04	31/03
Rugby Town	29/10	12/11	23/08	27/08	26/11	01/10	09/04	04/10	28/01	03/12	13/08	03/03	31/03	14/01	28/04	17/12	17/03	■	10/09	11/02	25/02	02/01
Slough Town	18/02	26/11	13/08	13/09	09/04	03/12	17/12	17/03	23/08	31/03	28/01	24/09	27/08	21/04	02/01	04/02	03/03	15/10	■	12/11	14/01	05/11
St. Neots Town	24/09	05/11	28/01	02/01	13/08	24/03	23/08	09/04	18/02	27/08	19/11	04/02	17/12	15/11	03/12	21/04	15/10	13/09	10/03	■	31/03	14/01
Uxbridge	29/08	04/02	07/04	15/11	13/09	28/04	10/03	29/10	15/10	19/11	31/12	18/02	07/01	14/04	21/01	20/08	26/12	24/09	16/08	10/12	■	24/03
Woodford United	20/08	17/03	29/10	07/01	12/11	25/02	11/02	03/03	14/04	01/10	07/04	26/12	10/09	31/12	11/10	01/10	10/12	29/08	28/04	16/08	26/11	■

Evo-Stik League Southern Division One South & West — 2011/2012 Fixtures

	Abingdon United	Bideford	Bishops Cleeve	Bridgwater Town	Cinderford Town	Clevedon Town	Didcot Town	Gosport Borough	Halesowen Town	Hungerford Town	Mangotsfield United	North Leigh	Paulton Rovers	Poole Town	Sholing	Stourport Swifts	Taunton Town	Thatcham Town	Tiverton Town	Wimborne Town	Yate Town
Abingdon United		18/02	24/09	21/04	07/04	19/11	26/12	04/02	13/09	16/08	15/10	29/08	20/08	31/12	14/04	10/12	13/08	15/11	05/11	10/03	24/03
Bideford	01/10		13/08	14/01	03/03	11/10	17/03	03/12	28/01	21/04	23/08	12/11	31/03	05/11	10/09	26/11	09/04	17/12	02/01	11/02	27/08
Bishops Cleeve	25/02	21/01		31/12	26/12	21/04	10/09	05/11	16/11	07/01	10/12	14/04	17/08	07/04	19/11	29/08	20/08	10/03	05/10	01/10	11/02
Bridgwater Town	29/10	16/08	27/08		07/01	11/02	28/04	20/08	31/03	21/01	03/03	26/11	03/12	17/03	25/02	12/11	02/01	10/09	09/04	04/10	17/12
Cinderford Town	03/12	15/11	09/04	23/08		05/11	13/08	15/10	02/01	13/09	24/09	04/02	21/04	18/02	28/01	14/01	31/03	19/11	27/08	24/03	10/03
Clevedon Town	17/03	04/02	29/10	13/09	28/04		12/11	26/11	17/12	24/09	14/01	18/02	02/01	15/10	13/08	23/08	27/08	03/12	03/03	28/01	09/04
Didcot Town	09/04	19/11	15/10	05/11	21/01	10/03		07/01	04/02	20/08	18/02	13/09	24/03	24/09	15/11	21/04	17/12	27/08	31/03	03/12	16/08
Gosport Borough	10/10	07/04	28/04	28/01	10/09	24/03	22/08		19/11	10/12	29/10	31/12	10/03	29/08	26/12	14/04	01/10	14/01	13/08	14/11	25/02
Halesowen Town	11/02	20/08	03/03	10/12	29/08	14/04	04/10	17/03		07/04	31/12	16/08	21/01	26/11	29/10	26/12	28/04	01/10	12/11	25/02	07/01
Hungerford Town	14/01	29/10	23/08	13/08	11/02	25/02	28/01	31/03	03/12		26/11	28/04	17/12	12/11	04/10	03/03	17/03	02/01	01/10	27/08	10/09
Mangotsfield United	10/09	07/01	31/03	14/11	25/02	15/08	01/10	21/04	27/08	24/03		21/01	09/04	20/08	10/03	05/11	03/12	03/10	11/02	17/12	02/01
North Leigh	02/01	10/03	17/12	24/03	04/10	01/10	11/02	27/08	14/01	05/11	13/08		19/11	21/04	23/08	28/01	25/02	09/04	10/09	31/03	03/12
Paulton Rovers	28/01	10/12	14/01	07/04	29/10	29/08	26/11	12/11	13/08	14/04	26/12	17/03		03/03	11/02	31/12	11/10	25/02	23/08	10/09	01/10
Poole Town	27/08	28/04	03/12	19/11	01/10	10/09	25/02	02/01	24/03	10/03	28/01	29/10	15/11		14/01	13/08	11/02	23/08	17/12	09/04	31/03
Sholing	17/12	15/10	17/03	24/09	20/08	21/01	03/03	09/04	21/04	04/02	12/11	07/01	14/09	17/08		18/02	26/11	31/03	03/12	02/01	05/11
Stourport Swifts	31/03	24/03	02/01	10/03	16/08	07/01	29/10	17/12	09/04	15/11	28/04	20/08	27/08	21/01	01/10		10/09	11/02	25/02	19/11	04/10
Taunton Town	21/01	26/12	28/01	29/08	10/12	31/12	14/04	18/02	05/11	19/11	07/04	24/09	04/02	12/09	24/03	15/10		21/04	14/01	26/09	14/11
Thatcham Town	03/03	14/04	12/11	15/10	17/03	07/04	31/12	17/08	18/02	29/08	04/02	26/12	24/09	07/01	10/12	14/09	29/10		26/11	28/04	20/08
Tiverton Town	28/04	29/08	04/02	26/12	31/12	15/11	10/12	21/04	10/03	18/02	13/09	15/10	07/01	14/04	07/04	24/09	16/08	24/03		29/10	19/11
Wimborne Town	12/11	13/09	18/02	04/02	26/11	20/08	07/04	03/03	24/09	31/12	14/04	10/12	15/10	26/12	29/08	17/03	07/01	05/11	21/04		21/01
Yate Town	26/11	31/12	13/09	14/04	12/11	26/12	14/01	24/09	23/08	15/10	29/08	07/04	18/02	10/12	28/04	04/02	03/03	28/01	17/03	13/08	

Football League Tables & Non-League Football Tables

AVAILABLE FROM WWW.SUPPORTERSGUIDES.COM

978-1-86223-218-1

978-1-86223-204-4

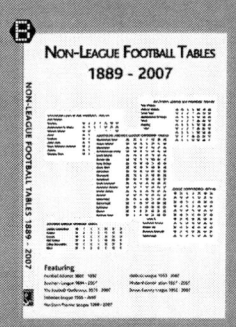

978-1-86223-162-7

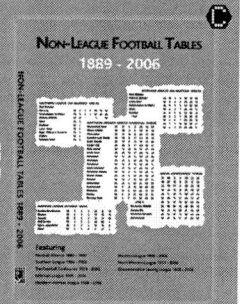

978-1-86223-144-3

978-1-86223-217-4

ALL NON-LEAGUE FOOTBALL TABLES BOOKS FEATURE THE FOLLOWING LEAGUES :

- Isthmian League
- Football Alliance
- Southern League
- Football Conference
- Northern Premier League

ADDITIONAL LEAGUES FEATURED :

- Sussex County League
- The Essex Senior League
- The Northern Counties East League
- The Central League
- The Midland Combination

- Hellenic League
- Midland Combination
- Devon County League

- Western League
- South Western League
- Gloucestershire County League

- United Counties League
- The East Midlands League
- The Welsh Premier League
- The United League
- The Central Amateur League
- The Central Combination
- The Lancashire League
- The Combination

£9.95 ISBN 978-1-86223-216-7

Supporters' Guides Series

This top-selling series has been published since 1982 and the new editions contain the 2010/2011 Season's results and tables, Directions, Photographs, Telephone numbers, Parking information, Admission details, Disabled information and much more.

THE SUPPORTERS' GUIDE TO PREMIER & FOOTBALL LEAGUE CLUBS 2012

This 28th edition covers all 92 Premiership and Football League clubs. **Price £7.99**

NON-LEAGUE SUPPORTERS' GUIDE AND YEARBOOK 2012

This 20th edition covers all 68 clubs in Step 1 & Step 2 of Non-League football – the Football Conference National, Conference North and Conference South. **Price £7.99**

SCOTTISH FOOTBALL SUPPORTERS' GUIDE AND YEARBOOK 2012

The 19th edition featuring all Scottish Premier League, Scottish League and Highland League clubs. **Price £6.99**

RYMAN FOOTBALL LEAGUE SUPPORTERS' GUIDE AND YEARBOOK 2012

This 2nd edition features the 66 clubs which make up the 3 divisions of the Isthmian League, sponsored by Ryman. **Price £6.99**

THE EVO-STIK LEAGUE SOUTHERN SUPPORTERS' GUIDE AND YEARBOOK 2012

This 2nd edition features the 66 clubs which make up the 3 divisions of the Southern Football League, sponsored by Evo-Stik. **Price £6.99**

THE EVO-STIK NORTHERN PREMIER LEAGUE SUPPORTERS' GUIDE AND YEARBOOK 2012

This 2nd edition features the 67 clubs which make up the 3 divisions of the Northern Premier League, sponsored by Evo-Stik. **Price £6.99**

THE SUPPORTERS' GUIDE TO WELSH FOOTBALL 2011

The enlarged 12th edition covers the 112+ clubs which make up the top 3 tiers of Welsh Football. **Price £8.99**

These books are available UK & Surface post free from –

Soccer Books Limited (Dept. SBL)
72 St. Peter's Avenue
Cleethorpes,   DN35 8HU
United Kingdom